Continue your adventure in history with three FREE historical novels from James Rada, Jr.

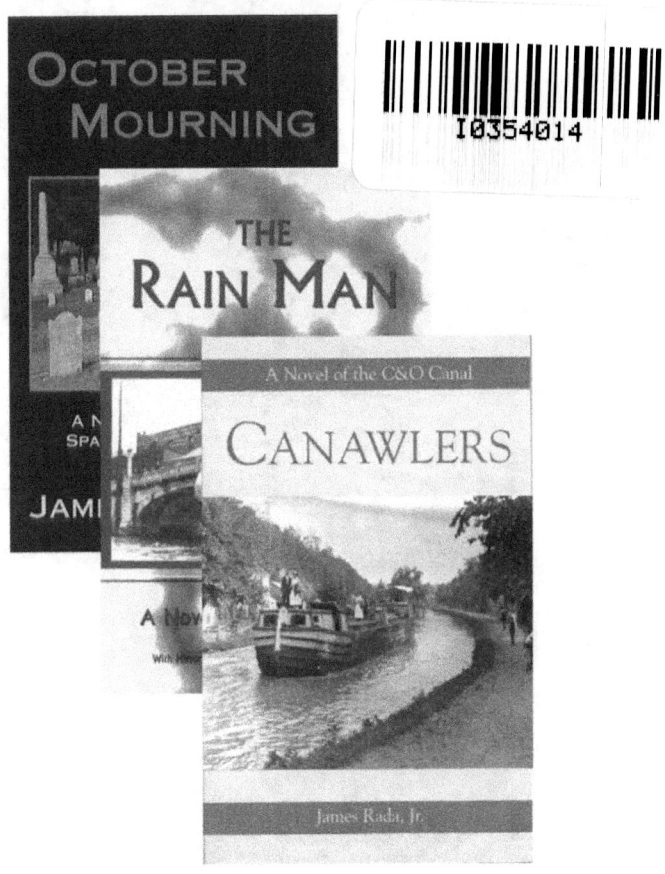

Visit *jamesrada.com / newsletter-email*
and enter your email
to receive your FREE novels.

CRITICAL ACCLAIM FOR THE WORKS OF JAMES RADA, JR.

The Last to Fall

"Authors Jim Rada and Richard Fulton have done an outstanding job of researching and chronicling this little-known story of those Marines in 1922, marking it as a significant moment in Marine Corps history."

- *GySgt. Thomas Williams*
Executive Director
U.S. Marine Corps Historical Company

"Original, unique, profusely illustrated throughout, exceptionally well researched, informed, informative, and a bit iconoclastic, "The Last to Fall: The 1922 March, Battles, & Deaths of U.S. Marines at Gettysburg" will prove to be of enormous interest to military buffs and historians."

- *Small Press Bookwatch*

Saving Shallmar

"But Saving Shallmar's Christmas story is a tale of compassion and charity, and the will to help fellow human beings not only survive, but also be ready to spring into action when a new opportunity presents itself. Bittersweet yet heartwarming, Saving Shallmar is a wonderful Christmas season story for readers of all ages and backgrounds, highly recommended."

- *Small Press Bookwatch*

Battlefield Angels

"Rada describes women religious who selflessly performed life-saving work in often miserable conditions and thereby gained the admiration and respect of countless contemporaries. In so doing, Rada offers an appealing narrative and an entry point into the wealth of sources kept by the sisters."

- *Catholic News Service*

Between Rail and River

"The book is an enjoyable, clean family read, with characters young and old for a broad-based appeal to both teens and adults. Between Rail and River also provides a unique, regional appeal, as it teaches about a particular group of people, ordinary working 'canawlers' in a story that goes beyond the usual coverage of life during the Civil War."

- *Historical Fiction Review*

Canawlers

"A powerful, thoughtful and fascinating historical novel, Canawlers documents author James Rada, Jr. as a writer of considerable and deftly expressed storytelling talent."

- *Midwest Book Review*

"James Rada, of Cumberland, has written a historical novel for high-schoolers and adults, which relates the adventures, hardships and ultimate tragedy of a family of boaters on the C&O Canal. ... The tale moves quickly and should hold the attention of readers looking for an imaginative adventure set on the canal at a critical time in history."

- *Along the Towpath*

October Mourning

"This is a very good, and very easy to read, novel about a famous, yet unknown, bit of 20th Century American history. While reading this book, in your mind, replace all mentions of 'Spanish Flu' with 'bird flu.' Hmmm."

- *Reviewer's Bookwatch*

SECRETS OF FRANKLIN COUNTY

Little-Known Stories & Hidden History
on Pennsylvania's State Line

Other books by James Rada, Jr.

Non-Fiction
- Battlefield Angels: The Daughters of Charity Work as Civil War Nurses
- Beyond the Battlefield: Stories from Gettysburg's Rich History
- Clay Soldiers: One Marine's Story of War, Art, & Atomic Energy
- Echoes of War Drums: The Civil War in Mountain Maryland
- How to Make a Living Freelance Writing
- The Last to Fall: The 1922 March, Battles & Deaths of U.S. Marines at Gettysburg
- Looking Back: True Stories of Mountain Maryland
- Looking Back II: More True Stories of Mountain Maryland
- No North, No South: The Grand Reunion at the 50th Anniversary of the Battle of Gettysburg
- Saving Shallmar: Christmas Spirit in a Coal Town

Black Fire Trilogy
- Smoldering Betrayal
- Strike the Fuse
- Frostburg Burning

Secrets Series
- Secrets of Allegany County: Little-Known Stories & Hidden History From Mountain Maryland
- Secrets of Catoctin Mountain: Little-Known Stories & Hidden History Along Catoctin Mountain
- Secrets of Garrett County: Little-Known Stories & Hidden History of Maryland's Westernmost County
- Secrets of the C&O Canal: Little-Known Stories & Hidden History Along the Potomac River
- Secrets of the Gettysburg Battlefield: Little-Known Stories & Hidden History from the Gettysburg Battlefield
- Secrets of the Washington County: Little-Known Stories & Hidden History Where Western Maryland Starts

Canawlers Series
- Between Rail and River
- Canawlers
- Lock Ready

Fiction
- October Mourning
- The Rain Man

SECRETS OF FRANKLIN COUNTY

Little-Known Stories & Hidden History
on Pennsylvania's State Line

by
James Rada, Jr.

LEGACY
PUBLISHING
A division of AIM Publishing Group

SECRETS OF FRANKLIN COUNTY: LITTLE-KNOWN STORIES AND HIDDEN HISTORY ON PENNSYLVANIA'S STATE LINE

Published by Legacy Publishing, a division of AIM Publishing Group.
Gettysburg, Pennsylvania.
Copyright © 2023 by James Rada, Jr.
All rights reserved.
Printed in the United States of America.
First printing: April 2023.

ISBN 978-1-7352890-7-6

This is a collection primarily of articles that have previously appeared in *Pennsylvania Magazine, The Chambersburg Public Opinion, The Gettysburg Times, F Magazine, and History Magazine.* In some cases where additional information is available the stories have been updated.

Cover design by Grace Eyler.

PUBLISHING

315 Oak Lane • Gettysburg, Pennsylvania 17325

CONTENTS

Franklin County, Pennsylvania 3
Interesting People 7
   The Fall of the Fly 9
   Richard Bard's Search to Rescue His Wife 15
   Patrick Gass: Explorer, Soldier, and Patriot 24
   When the Babe Came to Town 28
   Three Governors for Three States 33
      All from Franklin County
   Famous Inventor Dies in Waynesboro............................ 38
   A Hollywood Legend's 43
      Connection to Franklin County
   An English Duchess Born at Blue Ridge Summit 46
   Triplets Born Over Three Days 50
County Places 53
   Doctor vs. Doctor in Chambersburg Hospital Smear 55
   At Mont Alto, the Patients Ran the Hospital 61
   Paying the Rose Rent.. 65
   Building an Educational System in Franklin County 68
   County Gets a Vo-Tech School 71
   A Chambersburg Supermarket Was Ahead of Its Time . 75
Behind Bars 79
   Jailbreak! Not! 81
   Franklin County's Last Hanging...................................... 84
   Franklin County Jail Hosts Its First Wedding 91
Disease & Disaster 95
   Infant Paralysis Hits the County 97
   Don't Let the Flu Get You.. 100
   The Great 1936 Flood 109

A Pioneering Surgery Extends a Young Boy's Life.... 112
Frankenstorm, Nineteenth Century Style...................... 115
The Summer Blue Ridge Summit Burned 118
First Tornado in a Century Hits Chambersburg............ 121
The County at War 123
Chambersburg Takes Sides in the Civil War 125
Medal of Honor Purchased for a Dime 130
Love and Honor in a Time of War................................ 133
Farm Wife Kept Secret from Confederate Occupiers.. 139
Chambersburg's Role in the War of 1812 141
Odds & Ends 145
Boys of the Blue Ridge... 147
Brother vs. Brother Leads to Death 154
The Taste of Mountain Dew 160
A New Totem Pole for Totem Pole Playhouse 168
Waynesboro Residents Get Free Home Mail Delivery 171
More Radios than Bathrooms in County Farms 175
Getting Paid What He Was Worth................................ 178
George Washington Masonic Lodge Celebrates.......... 180
   Two Centuries and More
Chambersburg's Trolley Days 186
Hairy Memories 190
Acknowledgments 196
About the Author 198

Franklin County, Pennsylvania

Before Franklin County existed, it was part of Lancaster County in 1729, York County in 1749, and Cumberland County in 1750. However, it finally gained enough population to become its own county on September 9, 1784.

The United States had only recently won its own independence in 1781, and the population named the new county after Benjamin Franklin. Nowadays there are counties, towns, geologic formations, schools, businesses, streets, bridges, and more named after Franklin. Although twenty-four states also have counties named after Franklin, Pennsylvania was the third state to create a Franklin County. It was also in Franklin's home state.

Ebbert Springs, south of Greencastle, might be the oldest regularly occupied area in the county. It shows signs of prehistoric residents dating back to 10,000 B.C. It had a fort during the colonial era and the original stone house and spring house are still there. The Pennsylvania Historical and Museum Commission named it an archaeological super site and historic site.

The colonial settlers were primarily Scots-Irish, German, and Welsh. They began creating communities in Chambersburg, Greencastle, Mercersburg, Shippensburg, and Waynesboro.

"Our beginnings are easily traced to the year 1730 when Benjamin Chambers initiated a settlement at the confluence of the Conococheague and Falling Spring Creeks in the center of what is today Chambersburg," according to an article in Pennsylvania Heritage Magazine. "Within a few years the Scotch-Irish immigrants had homesteads and settlements throughout this area of the valley known as 'The Conococheague Settlement.'"

Once Franklin became a county, it needed to create its government infrastructure. The first courthouse was built in 1794 and the first jail in 1797.

The county marked its namesake with an eight-foot-tall, 250-pound statue of Benjamin Franklin coated in gold leaf. Frederick Mayer of Pittsburgh carved the statue in 1865, and it sat atop the county courthouse until 1991. At that time, it was removed for restoration. The statue on the courthouse now is a fiberglass replica.

The Benjamin Franklin statue (replica) about the Franklin County Courthouse in Chambersburg. Courtesy of Flickr.com.

Secrets of Franklin County

The county has been home to a number of notable people, but perhaps, the most famous to come from Franklin County is U.S. President James Buchanan. The man who would become the fifteenth President of the United States was born in a log cabin west of Mercersburg at Stony Batter in 1791.

The family moved to Mercersburg in 1796, and the home on Main Street where they lived and operated a general store is now the James Buchanan Pub & Restaurant.

Today, the county has nearly 156,000 residents and has thrived since the first 1790 Census when the population was nearly 16,000.

The Franklin County seal.

INTERESTING PEOPLE

The Fall of the Fly

Many a young boy loves to climb a tree, pushing the limits of gravity to see how high they can climb and enjoying the rush of adrenaline as the ground grows further and further away. Those boys grow up, though, and realize that if they should fall, they could be seriously injured.

Other boys just never seem to outgrow that urge to climb. They become daredevils. In the early 20th century, these climbers earned the nickname "Human Fly" or "Human Spider." They toured the country, accepting the challenge of climbing the tall buildings in any town. Although many of the famous Human Flies were active in the first couple decades of the 20th century, Human Fly John Ciampa climbed buildings in the 1940s and early 1950s, Human Fly George Willig climbed the World Trade Center in 1977 and Human Fly Rick Rojatt was a stunt rider in the 1970s.

In 1924, plans to have an open-air attraction from New York City entertain the crowds during Old Home Week in Chambersburg fell through so Human Fly George Oakley "one of the most daring of present-day human flies," according to *The Franklin Repository*, was invited as a replacement act. He was going to be performing in Hagerstown the week before, so it fit well with his schedule.

Oakley arrived for two evenings of performances on Saturday and Sunday, August 30 and 31. He did not look like would think of when they pictured a daredevil. He was a thirty-six-year-old man of medium height and a stout build.

Human Fly Harry Gardiner climbing a building. Courtesy of the Library of Congress.

He performed two daredevil feats for the crowds. For the first stunt, *The Franklin Repository*, "He will stand on his head on the front bumper rail of an auto, which will attain a speed of 30 miles an hour and suddenly stop. When it stops, Oakley will turn a somersault in the air, and land in the street right side up."

The second feat was just as, if not more, dangerous. He scaled the outside of the Chambersburg Trust building. "In scaling the walls he used a cane and an automobile inner tube. Someone would precede him to each story inside the building and hold the tube against the outside. The cane he used to hook onto the tube and then he would scale the wall to the window where he would wait for her until she had dropped the tube from the window above," *The Franklin Re-*

pository reported.

It was an exciting show that left people holding their breath and shutting their eyes when the tension became too great.

A human fly climbing the side of the Camden, New Jersey, courthouse. Courtesy of Wikimedia Commons.

During the Sunday night performance, thousands of people gathered to watch Oakley repeat his daring deeds. After his first stunt, his assistant, Anna Vivian Murray, urged him to rest a bit before scaling the tall bank building.

Oakley waved off her concerns and told her he was in a hurry and wanted to leave Chambersburg that evening. It would be at least 9 p.m. by the time that he finished.

"He kissed me and sent me upstairs with the tube," Murray said later.

Murray went into the building to wait at the second-floor window and Oakley soon began his climb. Minutes later, as he neared the fourth floor and hooked his cane on the inner tube, the crowd heard a "dull snap." The inner tube had broken, and the cane went flying off into the crowd.

"His fall was unbroken except by one man who rushed in in an attempt to save him," *The Repository* reported.

Oakley landed on his left side, smashing hard against the pavement. The crowd screamed and several women fainted. The police had trouble getting to Oakley because the crowd was so thick.

Four men lifted Oakley and put him into a cab. Murray, who said she was his wife, had reached his side by that time. Oakley was conscious. He asked for a priest and how far he had fallen.

"Only three stories. You're all right. George. You're more scared than hurt, you'll be all right," Murray told him.

This was not Oakley's first accident in his six years of daredevil climbing. His first accident had actually happened earlier in the year on July 4. Oakley fell 1½ stories while climbing a building in Scottsdale, Arizona. He had walked away from the fall with an injured left hand.

However, his climbing partner had died in a plane stunt a few weeks earlier. He had made a parachute jump and his chute had failed to open.

An examination at Chambersburg Hospital showed that Oakley had several broken bones, including lower vertebrae, his pelvis, ribs, left arm and his breast bone, with many of the bones being broken in multiple places. According to *The Franklin Repository*, his "nervous system suffering much from shock."

Oakley remained conscious for several hours. Father Noel of Corpus Christi Catholic Church arrived to deliver last rites. Throughout the night, Oakley's condition grew worse and Murray and a young boy stayed by his bedside.

Oakley died early the next morning. His body was taken to H. W. Cramer's for preparation for burial.

A copy of George Oakley's death certificate. Courtesy of Ancestry.com.

His wife, Clara, arrived from Cleveland, Ohio, which surprised many people because Oakley had introduced Murray as his wife and the young boy as his son. According to Oakley's WWI draft registration card, not only was Oakley married to Clara, but he had three children.

During the coroner's inquest, Murray admitted that she and Oakley hadn't been married, but had been planning to wed.

"I loved Oakley as I thought I could never love any man. We were to be married within a month. I never knew he was a married man, if he really was," she said.

More importantly, she told the jurors that Chambersburg had been the first time that she had held the inner tube for Oakley's climb. Chief Byers and Motorcycle Officer Suder tested the tube using the top of an open door at police headquarters to stretch the tube over. Suder said it broke under little strain.

A faulty or weak inner tube was the culprit. Coroner Shull ruled that death was accidental.

Richard Bard's Search to Rescue His Wife

Hannah McBride, a young girl who was at Bard's Mill, near Fairfield, on April 13, 1758, glanced out the door of the house. She screamed at the men were rushing the house. She turned to call out a warning to the others in the house, but it was too late.

Nineteen Delaware Indians rushed toward the house. Richard Bard, the mill owner, grabbed a pistol from its peg on the wall and fired at one of the Indians. The pistol misfired. The sight of it must have frightened the Indian and he ran off. Another Indian attacked Bard's cousin, Thomas Potter, with a knife. The two men struggled over the knife and Potter cut the Indian on the hand.

However, there were just too many attackers. Bard, his wife and son; Potter; Hannah; Frederick Ferrick, an indentured servant; two field hands and a young boy were all captured. The Indians killed and scalped Potter, most likely because he had injured one of the Delawares. The Indians also burned the mill down.

"We marched one after another at some distance," Bard wrote in his deposition. "At about seven miles they killed my child, which I discovered by seeing its scalp."

The party moved over South Mountain to the head of Falling Spring. They moved north of Fort Chambers and onto Rocky Spring and camped for the night near Fort McCord.

As they entered Path Valley on the second day, the Delawares discovered that a group of white men were pursuing them. The Delawares and their prisoners moved to the top of Tuscarora Mountain and threatened to kill the prisoners if the white pursuers reached them.

Marhall's Mill, built on the site of Bard's Mill near Fairfield, Pennsylvania. Scanned from *The Bard Family*.

Bard and Samuel Hunter, one of the field hands, sat down to rest at the top of the mountain "when an Indian without any previous warning sunk a tomahawk into the forehead of Samuel Hunter who was seated by my father and by repeated blows put an end to his existence He was then scalped and the Indians proceeding on their journey encamped that evening some miles on the north of Sideling Hill," according to the report of Archibald Barr.

They hiked on to Blair's Gap and while crossing Stoney Creek, the wind blew Bard's hat from the head of the Indian, who had taken it for his own. While the Indian went to recover it, Bard crossed the creek. The Indian returned and saw Bard had crossed. He was so angry that he pistol whipped Bard and nearly disabled him.

"And now reflecting that he could not possibly travel much further and that if this was the case he would be immediately put to death he determined to attempt his escape that night," Bard wrote.

Another thing pushing his decision was that his captors had painted half of his face red two days earlier. "This denoted that a council had been held and that an equal number were for putting him to death and for keeping him alive and that another council was to have taken place to determine the question," Bard wrote.

After the Indians laid down to rest, one of them dressed himself in Catherine Bard's gown to amuse his companions. While the Delawares relaxed, Richard Bard was sent to get water without his captors paying too close attention to him. When Bard got about 100 yards away, the Delawares realized he was getting away.

They chased after him, but he was gone. The Indians spent two days looking for him, but Richard Bard had made his getaway.

Richard Bard makes good his escape

Richard Bard had made his getaway from the Delaware Indians, who had captured his family at their mill near present-day Fairfield on April 13, 1758. He was one of the lucky ones. The Delawares had had killed two of their captives for no apparent reason. Five other people were still being held prisoner, including his wife.

Once the Indians discovered his escape, they searched for Bard, but he hid in a hollow log. Once the Indians had passed him by and were out of hearing range, Bard climbed out and ran off in the other direction.

"He traveled [across] the mountain pick[ing] berries and herbs to survive. His feet and legs were swollen, and his body was in a weak condition. The snow on the brush and leaves of the laurel made it impossible to walk, and he was [compelled] to creep on his hands and knees under the thick brush," according to L. Dean Calimer in *Franklin County Archives VII.*

A drawing from the poem "The Ballad of Richard Bard," which dramatized his escape from Indians and the rescue of his wife.

The Indians and their captives remained in the area for a day and night before making their way another twenty miles until they reached an Indian village. There, the squaws in the village severely beat Catherine Bard, Richard's wife.

"Now almost exhausted with fatigue she requested leave to remain at this place but was told she might if she preferred being scalped to proceeding," Archibald Bard, one of Richard and Catherine's children, wrote in *Incidents of border life*.

Instead, the Indians traveled to another village called Cususkey. Catherine and the others were beaten in this town as well. One man was even killed. "The Indians formed themselves into a circle round the prisoner and commenced by beating him some with sticks and some with tomahawks He was then tied to a post near a large fire and after being tortured sometime with burning coals they scalped him and put the scalp on a pole to bleed before his face A gun barrel was then heated red hot and passed over his body and with a red hot bayonet they pierced his body with many repetitions In this manner they continued torturing him singing and shouting until he expired," Archibald wrote.

Meanwhile, Richard was undergoing his own trials to stay alive. The fifth day after his escape, he got some protein in his diet when he killed and ate a rattlesnake.

Eight days after his escape, he found himself at a stream that he would have to wade. On the other side of the river, he found a path that led him to a settlement. He found himself facing three Indians. Instead of being the Delaware Indians who had captured him, they were friendly Cherokee Indians. They escorted Bard to Fort Lyttletown where he recovered from his experience.

Meanwhile, Catherine's ordeals went from being physically abused to being adopted as a sister by two Delaware Indians. Catherine was to replace their actual sister, who had died. Over the next few months, Catherine's new family traveled so much that she became ill and nearly died.

When she recovered, she got a glimpse of what the future

might hold for her when she met a woman she knew. "This woman had been in captivity some years and had an Indian husband by whom she had one child," Archibald wrote. "My mother reproved her for this but received for answer that before she had consented they had tied her to a stake in order to burn her."

The woman also told her that once captive women learned the Indian language, they either married one of the Delaware or were killed. Knowing this, Catherine played dumb and did not learn the language. She remained as the sister of the braves and was treated kindly.

Once recovered from his ordeal, Richard set out to free his family. He began seeking information about his wife and the Delawares, making many trips from his home to western Pennsylvania as he followed up on leads. As the weeks turned into years, he despaired at what had happened to his family, but he did not give up.

This determination was what would finally lead to his family being reunited.

Bard rescues his wife

After the Delaware Indians had captured the Bard Family in 1758 at their Fairfield mill, Richard Bard escaped his captivity after a few days. His wife, Catherine, wasn't so lucky. She remained a prisoner of the Indians.

The Delawares initially beat her, but once the war party arrived back in their village, two braves adopted Catherine as a sister. "She was treated during this time by her adopted relations with much kindness even more than she had reason to expect," Catherine's son, Archibald, wrote in *Incidents of Border Life*.

In the meantime, Richard Bard recovered from his ordeal and began hunting for his wife. The Indians had already killed one of his children, and he would not lose his wife. "From the time that my father was taken by the Indians until my mother was released he did little else than wander from place to place in quest of information respecting her and after he was informed where she was his whole mind bent upon contriving plans for her redemption," Archibald Bard wrote.

A model of Fort Duquesne. Courtesy of Wikimedia Commons.

Bard traveled to Fort Duquesne in the fall of 1758. A treaty had been signed with the Indians there and Bard went to meet with them to ask about his wife to see if he could find out where she had been taken.

Some of these Indians were the ones who raided Bard's mill and captured him, his family, and friends. "My father observed among them several who were when he was taken prisoner to these he discovered himself they professed not to know him on which he enquired of them they did not recollect having been at the taking of nine persons referring them to the time and place," Archibald Bard wrote.

When Bard left the Indians and returned to Fort Duquesne, a young man followed him, and warned Bard that after he had left, the Indians had said "that they never had a stronger desire for any thing than to have sunk the tomahawk into his head and that they had agreed to kill him on his return next day," according to Archibald Bard. The young Indian warned Bard not to return the next day if he wanted to live.

A Delaware Indian. Courtesy of Wikimedia Commons.

Instead, Bard traveled with a wagon convoy to Fort Bedford, where he met an Indian named Captain White Eyes who was friends with the Moravian missionaries in the area. A few miles from Fort Bedford, the Indians with the convoy got drunk. One of the wagon drivers was scalped and Bard was once again captured.

"Captain White Eyes was soon under the influence of

liquor, and told Bard if he tried to escape, he would be shot. He told Bard that he knew that he had escaped from the Delawares before," to L. Dean Calimer in *Franklin County Archives VII.*

White Eyes fired at Bard, but he jumped behind a tree. Bard then moved around the tree to keep it between himself and the Indian. The other Indians found this amusing until one of them finally grew tired of it and disarmed White Eyes.

White Eyes them grabbed a stick and began beating Bard, but Bard made his way to a horse and escape.

Following up on information about his wife being was at the Indian village of Shamokin (Sunbury, PA), Bard made his way to Pittsburgh. He wrote a letter to his wife saying that if her adopted friends would bring her to Pittsburgh and release her, he would pay 40 pounds. Bard hoped that even if they wouldn't release her, some other Indians would hear about the reward offer and free her.

While the Indians who had adopted Catherine Bard were willing to free her, they feared they wouldn't be paid the bounty.

"To allay their suspicions he told them to keep him as a hostage, while they sent Mrs. Bard into the town with an order for the money. This put the savages in good humor, and they took them into the town, where the money was paid and his wife was released," Calimer wrote.

Catherine had been a captive of the Delawares for two years and five months.

Following her release, the Bards returned to Franklin County and bought a plantation near Williamson.

Bard went on to serve in the Revolutionary War. He was also a member of the Pennsylvania Convention in 1787, which was the group of Pennsylvanians who were asked to ratify the U.S. Constitution in the Commonwealth.

Patrick Gass: Explorer, Soldier, and Patriot

Patrick Gass was a native son of Franklin County, but the impact of his life stretched far beyond the borders of the county and Commonwealth of Pennsylvania.

"Before he died on April 2nd, 1870 at the age of almost 99 years, great cities had been built and untold wealth found in the land he had helped discover. During the War of 1812 he fought in some of the bloodiest battles of the campaign on the Canadian border, and at the age of 63, after a lifetime spent in the service of his country, he married a girl of 20, whom he survived many years. Born before the Revolution, he lived to see this country grow from the original thirteen colonies to 38 states; he voted at the election of 18 presidents from Washington to Grant who served during his lifetime. Four great wars... the Revolution, the War of 1812, the Mexican and Civil were fought, in addition to numerous Indian battles. It is little wonder that Patrick Gass led such an adventurous life, for he was born June 12th, 1771, at Falling Springs, not far from the present town of Chambersburg, Pennsylvania, then on the Western frontier of civilization," the introduction to a 1958 edition of Gass's journal reads.

As a youth, Gass's family moved around a lot due to his father's wanderlust. He began his military career in 1792 as a militia member serving under General Anthony Wayne (for whom Waynesboro, Pennsylvania, is named) and fighting Indians in at Bennett's Fort in Wheeling, Virginia (now West

Virginia).

Following his stint in the military, Gass moved to Mercersburg, Pennsylvania, and became a carpenter's apprentice. While there, he worked on the home of James Buchanan, Sr., and came to know Buchanan's son who would become the President of the United States.

Patrick Gass.

Gass joined the Continental Army in 1799 and served under General Alexander Hamilton until 1800. He rejoined the army in 1803 and, while serving, he volunteered to travel with Lewis and Clark on their expedition. Gass served as a carpenter on the journey and was promoted to sergeant. He helped build winter quarters, dugout canoes, and wagons on the journey. He even commanded a large portion of the expedition for a short time while Lewis and Clark led smaller side excursions.

During the journey, Gass maintained a journal. His language was rough and difficult to read for portions because of Gass's limited education, so he had a schoolteacher, David McKeehan, edit it for publication. The journal was published the year after Gass's return in 1806 and became a great primary source about the Lewis and Clark expedition.

He was the first person from the expedition group to publish his story. The book sold well in the United States and was also translated into German and French for foreign editions.

A few years after he returned, Gass fought in the War of 1812. General Andrew Jackson drafted him to fight Creek Indians in the South. "But this assignment did not suit Gass. He wanted to hear the roar of the big guns, and he was released when he accepted a cash bonus of $100 to enlist in the regular army for five years," according to Gass's journal introduction.

By 1814, he was at the Niagara frontier, though his unit arrived a few hours late to take part in the Battle of Chippewa.

"However, Gass saw plenty of fighting during the next few weeks. He received his baptism of fire from the big guns he wanted to hear at Lundy's Lane on July 25th. He was one of the gallant 300 who, led by Colonel James Miller, charged and captured the British battery after a desperate hand-to-hand struggle during the night," according to the journal introduction.

Gass lost an eye during this battle. Though legend has it he lost it chopping wood later, he presented a petition to the U.S. Congress in 1851 seeking a pension because he had lost his eye in battle.

When the Civil War broke out, the ninety-one-year-old Gass tried to enlist in the Union Army. He was so insistent about it that he had to be removed from the recruiting station, according to the *Wisdom of History* by Rufus J. Fears.

When Gass died in 1870 in Wellsburg, West Virginia, he was the last living member of the Lewis and Clark expedition.

When the Babe Came to Town

People were buying up so many tickets for a single baseball game that temporary seating needed to be added to Henninger Field in 1929. Even then, it didn't look like it would be enough to seat the record crowd.

Henninger Field, at the corner of Vine Street and Riddle Alley in Chambersburg, Pennsylvania, had been built as Wolf Park in 1895. It had been renamed in 1920 in honor of Clay Henninger, the Chambersburg businessman who formed the Chambersburg Maroons baseball team. The New York Yankees purchased the Maroons in 1929, which is what led to the Yankees coming to town for an exhibition game.

It wasn't so much the Yankees' arrival that caused all the excitement in town, though. Babe Ruth was coming to Chambersburg. Despite the Yankees being the reigning World Series champions, the Babe was the only player who was named in the advertisements for the May 31, 1929, exhibition game. The ad headlines read: "N.Y. Yankees with Babe Ruth vs. Chambersburg Young Yanks." Even the great Lou Gehrig wasn't mentioned in the ads.

A second game between Chambersburg and Martinsburg was on the schedule as well, although no one would remember watching that game. They came to see baseball's living legend play.

The Yankees reserved twelve double rooms and a sample room at the Hotel Washington, though they weren't spending the night. On game day, the Yankees bus arrived from Washington, D.C. just after noon. The seventeen players, coaches and entourage headed into the hotel to rest up for the 3:30 p.m. game.

Because of the big turnout expected at the game, most of the town's businesses had decided to close down for the afternoon so that the clerks and employers could "meet and swap peanuts on the bleachers," according to the *Chambersburg Public Opinion*.

Babe Ruth was known for the close connection he had with children. Courtesy of Wikimedia Commons.

The team rested up in their rooms and left for Henninger Field at 2:15 p.m. The crowds were already waiting outside of the hotel for a chance to meet Ruth. As the Babe climbed into a car to leave, kids swarmed around it, "then one braver than the rest, walked to the car and shot out his hand to the famous ball player. Ruth seized it with avidity and a moment later the remaining children, emboldened by their companion, surged around the car to receive a handshake," the newspaper reported.

Ruth was used to the attention. It was part of the connection that he shared with his fans. When the caravan of cars reached the ball field, the players found around 2,600 fans waiting for them, including people who hadn't been out to see a baseball game in years.

"The big fellow's magnetism drew the crowd to him from the time he entered the park and started his warming up exercises along the right-field bleachers and after the game he was the center of a wildly admiring crowd at the rear of the grandstand," the *Public Opinion* reported.

The crowd of 2,600 was the largest turnout ever at Henninger Field. All the seats were filled and people were standing along the fence. Temporary bleachers were brought in and placed on land owned by Augustus Wolf.

Ruth's young fans lined the temporary fencing around the field on the right side, hoping for a chance to talk to the Babe while he played first base. To reward his young fans, he would toss his baseballs to the boys after his between-inning warm-ups. That would send them scrambling in a heap for the ball. He also exchanged a lot of good-natured banter with the crowd between innings.

During the second inning, boys shifted around to find a seat on the makeshift bleachers that had been added to accommodate the crowd, "but within a few moments fans who had a view of the structure were horrified to see it collapse with its human weight. Boards flew in the air amid screams of the youngsters who a moment before had been watching the game."

One young boy was injured slightly in the crash, but not enough that the game had to be postponed for a significant amount of time.

Ruth hit his only home run of the game in the fifth inning. It came with Gehrig and Andrew Durst on base.

Babe Ruth warming up before a baseball game. Courtesy of the Library of Congress.

"The ball soared high and far over the centerfield fence, traveling about 400 feet," according to the *Public Opinion*.

Though it was Ruth's only home run during the game, he hit many more over the fence in his pre-game warm-up, including one that landed in the stone quarry beyond the right-field fence.

Following the Yankees 8-1 win over Chambersburg's

Blue Ridge League team, "he autographed baseballs until he was threatened with writer's cramp."

When he could finally make his way out of Henninger's Field, he was met with even more fans.

"After he had autographed more baseballs, he had to shove and push his way to a waiting taxi and then some of his useful admirers swung onto the runningboard of the car to shake his hand."

Back at the hotel, the Yankees packed up their things and boarded the bus to go onto Chicago and their next game.

Three Governors for Three States All from Franklin County

The front page of the November 3, 1915, *Public Opinion* carried all the local and state election returns. The women's suffrage vote was a hot button issue for this election, with most of the stories mentioning not only who won a particular race, but how the suffrage vote went.

Lost amid those stories was a minor story with a headline that took up nearly as much room as the story itself, "Franklin Co. Boy Elected Governor in Massachusetts."

Republican Samuel W. McCall had defeated the incumbent governor, David Walsh, "by a plurality of about about 25,000 although Walsh carried Boston," according to the *Public Opinion*.

The newspaper notes that "Franklin County is interested in the above because Mr. McCall was born and raised here. He spent his boyhood with his uncle, Tine Elliott, who lived along Warm Spring Road."

That McCall's family was from Franklin County and that he spent time here with his uncle is certain, but what is less certain is whether he was actually "born and raised here."

Most sources state that McCall was born in East Providence, Pennsylvania, in Bedford County, though a few list it as New Providence, Pennsylvania, in Lancaster County.

McCall was born on February 28, 1851, the sixth of eleven children his parents would have. His great-grandfather on his mother's side was Ennion Elliott, Franklin County High

Sheriff. "Old residents of Chambersburg, the shire town, were long in the habit of relating stories of his industry in politics. Early in the morning he would set out on horseback equipped with saddlebags, and canvass the voters of his county," Lawrence Evans wrote in his 1916 biography of McCall.

Massachusetts Governor Samuel W. McCall.

Evans notes that McCall's family moved to Illinois while McCall was still a child, but this would not have prevented him from visiting his uncle at times.

McCall attended college at Dartmouth and graduated in 1874 when he began to study law. He was admitted to the bar in 1875 and began work in Worcester, Massachussetts, and later Boston.

He would also serve as the editor of the *Boston Daily Advertiser* for a time.

McCall began his political career in 1888 as a member of the Massachusetts House of Representatives. He was also a representative in 1889 and 1892. He was elected to Congress in 1893 and served for twenty years. He returned to Boston in 1913 to take up his law practice again.

However, his political career was not over and he was elected as governor with future president Calvin Coolidge as his lieutenant governor. He served only a single term before retiring from public service.

McCall died on November 4, 1923, at seventy-two and is buried in Wildwood Cemetery in Winchester, far from the land of his birth.

Robert McClelland

Robert McClelland was born in Greencastle, Pennsylvania, on August 1, 1807. Although his father was a doctor, he chose to enter law and was admitted to the Pennsylvania bar in 1831. He practiced law in Pittsburgh before moving west into what was the Territory of Michigan at the time.

Michigan became the twenty-sixth state in the Union in 1837. McClelland had been a member of the constitutional convention for Michigan two years earlier and remained active in state affairs.

He served on the board of regents for the University of Michigan while maintaining a law practice in the state.

The people of the state elected him in the state house for the first time in 1838, and by 1843, he was the speaker of the Michigan House of Representatives. He served as the mayor of Monroe in 1841 and the U.S. House of Representatives in 1842 where he served until 1849.

In 1851, McClelland was elected the ninth governor of Michigan. He resigned as governor in 1853 to serve as the U.S. Secretary of the Interior under Franklin Pierce.

When a fellow Franklin Countian, James Buchanan, was inaugurated as president in 1857, McClelland retired from public office and went back to practicing law.

Michigan Governor Robert McClelland.

William Findlay

The third governor from Franklin County was William Findlay. He was a native of Mercersburg, born on June 20, 1768. He and his siblings became active in politics at all levels.

Findlay began life as a farmer, but he soon took an interest in politics. He served as a brigade inspector for the Pennsylvania Militia and studied law. He also served in the Pennsylvania House of Representatives and as the state treasurer.

In 1817, he was nominated as governor in Pennsylvania's first open convention. He was elected in December of that year and served for three years until 1820. He was the first governor to govern from Harrisburg, which became the state capital of Pennsylvania in 1812. Because the capitol building was under construction at the time, he worked much of the time from his home.

Following his time as governor, he returned to the state legislature until he became a U.S. senator and treasurer of the U.S. Mint.

Governors for three states, who were members of two political parties, from one Pennsylvania county.

Pennsylvania Governor William Findlay.

Famous Inventor Dies in Waynesboro

Peter Geiser could have been the patron saint of farmers and Waynesboro, Pennsylvania. He made farmers' lives easier and brought prosperity to Waynesboro. When Geiser died in 1901, both mourned his passing.

"In the home from which he often looked over the town he had done much to build up by the invention of the grain separator and the prosperity of which had been the ruling passion of his life, Peter Geiser died suddenly last evening," *The Public Opinion* announced on its front page on March 20, 1901.

Geiser had been born in Washington County, Maryland, near Smithsburg, 75 years earlier. His mother's maiden name was Singer from the family that invented the sewing machine, so it is probably safe to say that inventing was in Geiser's blood.

He showed that inclination from a young age as he took to whittling and woodcarving. This led to him creating his own workshop where he could build contraptions and figure other ones out. In that workshop between 1848 and 1850, Geiser developed what would become his life's work. He patented his first grain thresher, separator, cleaner, and conveyor in October 1852.

Geiser entered his thresher in a competition at the Hagerstown Fair in 1854 and took first prize against other threshers. He then took his invention to competitions in Ohio and

Indiana, where his thresher and separator also won the top prizes.

"There is no question that Peter Geiser was one of the great inventors of the age, and should rank along with Cyrus McCormick, John Deere and a host of others," wrote W. J. Eshleman in *Steam Traction*.

Peter Geiser.

In 1860, Geiser moved his new manufacturing company to Waynesboro. When he opened his business, Geiser ran this advertisement in the newspaper:

"The undersigned having removed his foundry and machine shop to Waynesboro where he is better prepared to carry on his business in all its various branches than formerly would call the attention of persons in want of anything in his line as he is fully prepared to make to order and on short notice, steam engines, grist and sawmills, gearing, shafting and pulleys, iron bridges, cast iron water wheels, iron kettles, stoves, and plow castings, also cast and wrought iron kettles, stoves, and plow castings, also cast and wrought iron for steam or water, and brass castings of every description; in a word he is prepared to do everything usually done in a foundry and a machine shop. Having supplied himself with the latest improved machinery, such as lathes, boring, planing and drilling machines, persons can rely upon having their work done in the most satisfactory manner. He is also prepared to manufacture to order machinery for wood, such as tongueing and grooving machines for flooring, surface, tenant, moulding machines, etc. He also manufactures 'GEISER'S PATENT SELF-REGULATING GRAIN SEPARATORS' with latest improvements. Also the triple-geared horsepower arranged for running on wheels. All persons in want of these machines will give in their orders at an early date to have them secured."

The last Peerless Engine, one of Peter Geiser's patented machines that threshed, separated, cleaned, and conveyed grain. It is owned by Samuel G. Stoltzfus of White Horse, Pennsylvania. Courtesy of W. J. Eshleman.

By the end of the year, 150 Geiser threshers had been built in eight locations. With the outbreak of the Civil War, Geiser Manufacturing hit hard times, which it barely survived.

Following the war, the company began a period of expansion. New shops were built on Broad Street in Waynesboro in 1866 and the company went public in 1869. The stock offering raised $134,600, and new buildings were constructed. In its first year as a public company, Geiser Manufacturing employed 175 men and sold 400 machines. This is 100 more than had been sold during all the years of the Civil War combined.

Tragedy struck in 1882 when a fire destroyed the company's buildings in Waynesboro. However, the company rebuilt and began expanding again. This time, the expansion came mainly through the purchase of other manufacturing companies.

In March 1901, Geiser's son-in-law found his father-in-law on the couch "in the throes of death," according to *The Public Opinion*. The son-in-law tried to help, but Geiser died before a doctor arrived.

"He was a genius of rare ability and magnificent faith in the utility and ultimate success of the separator. No sacrifice was too great for him to make and no obstacle too big for him to overcome. He was a good citizen and esteemed by all who knew him…. His genius has brought much of its population to Waynesboro and contributed vastly to its wealth," the *Blue Ridge Zephyr* wrote of Geiser after his death.

He was survived by his wife of forty-six years, Mary, and ten of their eleven children. Geiser was buried on March 20 in Green Hill Cemetery in Waynesboro.

Geiser Manufacturing continued after Geiser's death, though it sold to Emerson-Brantingham Co. of Rockford, Illinois, in 1912. A group of Waynesboro investors purchased the company from Emerson-Brantingham Co. in 1925.

The Great Depression did the company in. Geiser Manufacturing went into bankruptcy in 1939. M. N. Landay Co. of Pittsburgh purchased the assets in 1940. The new owners were removing the old equipment when another fire struck, destroying the company. "The glow of the fire could be seen for over forty miles," according to *Steam Traction*.

A Hollywood Legend's Connection to Franklin County

While it's well-known that legendary actor James Stewart hailed from Pennsylvania, what's not as well-known is that he had personal and family connections in Franklin County.

James Stewart was born on May 20, 1908, in Indiana, Pennsylvania, about 120 miles west of Chambersburg. He was one of three children, but the only son of Elizabeth and Alexander Stewart.

Though the Stewart family's roots in Indiana County date back to 1772, they emigrated there from Franklin County when James Stewart's third great-grandfather, Fergus Moorhead, arrived.

"After Fergus was captured by Indians in July 1776, his wife and three children returned to Franklin County. He was held captive for 11 months," according to the Heritage Center in Chambersburg, Pennsylvania.

Stewart was raised with small-town values in a Presbyterian home in Indiana.

"James was a bright and lively boy, who liked to build model airplanes and radio crystal sets, who enjoyed playing with chemistry sets, took pride in being a Boy Scout, dabbled in magic games in the parlor and, most of all, admired his somewhat gruff but full-of-life father," Tony Thomas wrote in *A Wonderful Life: The Films and Career of James Stewart.*

When Stewart turned fifteen, his parents enrolled him in the Mercersburg Academy.

Mercersburg Academy began as Marshall College in 1836. Marshall College moved to Lancaster, Pennsylvania, in

1853, but the preparatory department remained in Mercersburg. It was called Mercersburg College from 1865 to 1893 when it became the Mercersburg Academy. That first year, the academy had forty students and four instructors on four acres of leased ground.

While attending the school, Stewart took part in the glee club, choir, debate, John Marshall Literary Society and the yearbook club. He also played on the football and track teams. On weekend afternoons, he would go to see movies playing at the Star Theater in Mercersburg, according to the Heritage Center.

James Stewart as a young man.

During his summer breaks, Stewart would return home and work odd jobs. He was a brick loader for a construction company, magician's assistant, and line painter with highway road crews.

In 1928, Stewart made his first appearance onstage at Mercersburg as Buquet in *The Wolves,* according to Mark Eliot in *Jimmy Stewart: A Biography.* It was the same year that he graduated in a class of 103.

Secrets of Franklin County

From Mercersburg, Stewart went onto Princeton University, where he studied architecture and found his true calling as an actor. Not only did Stewart become an Academy-Award-winning actor and Hollywood legend, he also made a name for himself as an Air Force pilot. He flew dozens of successful bombing raids during World War II, reaching the rank of colonel and later brigadier general in the Air Force Reserve.

The Stewart family also had other connections with Franklin County. Stewart's son, Michael, attended the Mercersburg Academy and one of his ancestors, Elizabeth Ruth Jackson, graduated from Wilson College, according to the Heritage Center.

The Mercersburg Academy continues to educate youth. Academy alumni live in all fifty states and seventy-six countries. According to the Mercersburg Academy website, alumni include three Medal of Honor recipients, fifty-four Olympians (including twelve gold medalists), seven Rhodes Scholars, eleven Fulbright Scholars, one Nobel Laureate, two Academy Award winners, two Golden Globe winners, and one Emmy Award winner.

An English Duchess is Born at Blue Ridge Summit

When Alice Montague and Teakle Wallis Warfield married in 1895, Alice was already pregnant and Teakle was dying. He had tuberculosis, which is probably why they traveled to Blue Ridge Summit in the summer of 1896. Besides being a popular summer resort, it was also believed that the fresh air at higher elevations was good for a person's health.

The Warfields stayed in Square Cottage at the Monterey Inn in Blue Ridge Summit. It was the town's largest hotel at the time and featured not only a central building but also wooden cottages.

While staying there, Alice went into labor and Bessie Wallis Warfield was born on June 19, 1896, seven months after her parents had been married in Baltimore.

Wallis would never remember her father, though. He died on Nov. 15 of that year before she was even five months old.

Wallis's uncle, Solomon Davies Warfield, took in Wallis and her mother. He was the postmaster of Baltimore and a wealthy bachelor. They lived in a four-story row home on Preston Street in Baltimore.

Alice Warfield married John Freeman Rasin in 1908. Wallis was confirmed in 1910 at the Christ Episcopal Church.

Between 1912 and 1914, she attended the most-expensive school in Maryland, Oldfields School. According to Charles

Higham in his book, *Mrs. Simpson*, this is where she became friends with Renée du Pont, a member of the DuPont Family, and Mary Kirk, whose family founded Kirk Silverware.

Wallis Simpson.

Wallis married Earl Winfield Spencer, Jr., a Navy aviator, in 1916. The marriage was marked by long periods apart, as Spencer was stationed at different postings. She began traveling in Europe and China during the 1920s. She also began several affairs with men she met during her travels.

Higham wrote that an Italian diplomat said of Wallis, "Her conversation was brilliant and she had the habit of bringing up the right subject of conversation with anyone she came in contact with and entertaining them on that subject."

Not surprisingly, Wallis and Spencer divorced at the end of 1927. She was already having an affair with a shipping executive named Ernest Aldrich Simpson. He divorced his wife, Dorothea, to marry Wallis on July 21, 1928. They lived in England, which is where Wallis came to meet Edward, Prince of Wales, at different house parties hosted by members of the upper class.

It is believed that Wallis and Prince Edward began an affair in 1934 while his current mistress was traveling abroad. By the end of the year, he was deeply in love with Wallis and she with him.

However, his family was against the pairing, primarily because of Wallis's marital history. Things became even more complicated when George V died on January 20, 1936. Edward became Edward VIII, the king of England. He watched the proclamation of his accession with Wallis from a window in St. James's Palace, which was a break from royal protocol.

Heavier attention now fell on Edward's relationship with Wallis. Most of British royalty seemed against the relationship.

When it became apparent that Edward wanted to marry Wallis, it became a legal issue because the Church of England, which the British monarch headed, did not permit the remarriage of divorced people with living spouses.

To make matters worse, Wallis would be a two-time divorcee, since she had filed for divorce from her second husband on October 27, 1936.

As the English public became more aware of the affair, it became a scandal. Under pressure from the British government, Wallis announced that she was willing to give up her newest love, but Edward was not ready.

He abdicated the throne on December 10, 1936, and his

brother, the Duke of York, became King George VI the next day.

Edward addressed his country via radio and said, "I have found it impossible to carry the heavy burden of responsibility, and to discharge my duties as King as I would wish to do, without the help and support of the woman I love."

He and Wallis stayed apart until her divorce was finalized in May 1937. She took on her maiden name, and the couple reunited. They married on June 3, 1937, and the child born at Blue Ridge Summit became the Duchess of Windsor.

Triplets Born Over Three Days

In 1886, Emma Catherine Tracey of Fountaindale gave birth three days in a row.

Mabel Viola Tracey was born around noon on April 4, weighing 6 lbs. Her sister, Edith Grace Tracey, was born the following day around noon, also weighing 6 lbs. Finally, Bessie Barton Tracey was born on April 6 around 6 p.m. and weighed 7 lbs. Dr. Abram Pierce Beaver of Fairfield, Pennsylvania, delivered the children.

A total of fifty-four hours separated the births.

Because of the expense involved with raising triplets, the Traceys took pictures of the triplets on Aug. 26 and began selling them as postcards for 25 cents each (about $11 in today's dollars). One side of the card had the picture of the children. The other side had information about them and their unusual birth. However, it misspelled Mabel's name as Mable and listed Bessie's birth time as 4 p.m.

The card also mentioned that Emma had been born with only one arm. Her health seemed perfect otherwise. Not only did she survive the birth, she lived until 1949 and was 91 years old when she died.

The girls lived long lives, marrying and having children of their own. When they were seventy-nine years old in 1965, newspapers reported that they were the oldest living triplets in Pennsylvania, and possibly, the country.

Bessie, the youngest of the triplets, was the first to die. She passed away on February 24, 1966, shortly before turning eighty. The cause of her death was listed as "Ovarian carcinoma & metastases."

The Tracey triplets. Left to right: Mabel, Bessie, and Edith. Courtesy of Findagrave.com.

Mabel and Edith died the following year on Jan. 17 and Mar. 20, respectively. Mabel's cause of death was listed as "Recurrent myocardial infarction & hypertensive cardiovascular, due to severe disease and thrombus in the left ventricle." Edith's cause of death was listed as "Myocardial infarction, acute, due to [*illegible*] heart disease and generalized arteriosclerosis."

The sisters are all buried in Green Hill Cemetery in Waynesboro.

Nowadays, triplets make up only about five percent of births, and fertility drugs have boosted that number. In 1886, it was even less frequent, so the Tracey girls began life as a rarity. As the *Waynesboro Record Herald* noted in 1950, "The rarity of their births 64 years ago was made more significant last month when three babies were born on consecutive days, but within a much shorter span of time, to a woman in Jonesville, Louisiana. When this phenomena was learned, press associations over the world proclaimed the three-day birth series as having occurred perhaps 'the first time in medical history.'"

But it had happened before.

County Places

Doctor vs. Doctor in a Chambersburg Hospital Smear

The rumors had been running rampant through Chambersburg, Pennsylvania, for months. If you went to Chambersburg Hospital for treatment, you were gambling with your life. The doctors and staff there were unethical and incompetent. This wasn't just idle rumor-mongering either. It was Franklin County doctors who were telling their patients this.

It reached the point that the Franklin County Medical Society backed the charges by some of its members. The Chambersburg Hospital Board of Directors launched an intensive investigation into the accusations. The hospital operated as a public charity, which meant that the directors were community businessmen. Their primary concern was to ensure that good healthcare was available to everyone in the community, regardless of their ability to pay. The original hospital opened on South Main Street in 1895 with three private rooms and two three-bed wards (one for men and one for women). However, through the hard-working fundraising efforts of the community, a new thirty-five-bed hospital was opened on Lincoln Way East that included larger wards for charity patients.

The investigating committee submitted its report to the directors in February 1909. *The Public Opinion* published the entire report, word for word, because it was a topic of interest to everyone in the community and the editors wanted to present the report with no bias. It took up roughly three full pages of the newspaper.

The report shows that the charges against the hospital doctors and staff came primarily from doctors who were not associated with the hospital. The committee appointed by the hospital directors took sworn statements not only from the accusers, but the accused and also the patients who were involved with the charges. The members also poured over documents, articles, telegrams and letters attempting to discern the truth.

Chambersburg Hospital. Photo courtesy of the Franklin County Historical Society – Kittochtinny.

In one instance, John Ott of Shippensburg said Dr. J. Bruce McCreary told him and his wife that a specialist would come from Philadelphia to perform a $300 operation for $100. Typically, visiting doctors who came to perform operations for paying patients would also operate on charity patients who needed a specialist's skills. Ott said that Dr.

Charles Palmer, a doctor at the hospital, performed the operation without Ott's knowledge and Mrs. Ott died a few weeks later.

McCreary told the committee that Ott had been informed every step of the way, including that Palmer would be the operating surgeon. There had been a possibility that when a specialist came in from Philadelphia, he would have performed the surgery, but Mrs. Ott's condition advanced too quickly and she needed the surgery sooner than a visiting specialist would be available. However, McCreary, who was not affiliated with the hospital, considered Palmer a specialist and more than capable of performing the operation. All of which McCreary said Ott knew.

As to why Ott might be lying about the circumstances of his wife's operation, Palmer added, "He owes me from fifty to one hundred dollars and it is simply the manner he has taken to get out of paying me and paying another other fees in connection with the case."

Palmer had been treating Mrs. Ott for two years for the condition that ultimately killed her and hadn't received a dime in payment. This also added credence to the fact that it shouldn't have surprised Ott that Palmer operated on Mrs. Ott.

A patient's uncle leveled another charge against the hospital. McCreary told the committee, "The complaint of the uncle of this young lady was that the Hospital was too cold. There was no foundation for the complaint and the patient would come back here to-morrow if her uncle would allow her."

Other accusations against the hospital dealt with billing issues wherein the doctors and staff were accused of graft. These turned out to be either the accuser's complete misunderstanding of the situation or a problem that the accusing doctor created himself by not filling out paperwork properly. The fact that "the enemies of the Hospital have 'unearthed,' as they say, about a dozen cases on which to prefer charges—some serious, most of them utterly trivial—with the apparent intention of discrediting and thereby curtailing the usefulness of the institution or of degrading members of their own profession," soon became apparent in additional accusations.

Chambersburg Hospital cleared of charges of wrongdoing

In 1909, Chambersburg Hospital was under attack from its own. Franklin County doctors accused the doctors and staff at the hospital of gross incompetence and unethical practices. The Chambersburg Hospital Board of Directors investigated the accusations, and the investigating committee submitted its report in March 1909. *The Public Opinion* published the entire report, word for word. It took up roughly three full pages of the newspaper.

Doctors who were not associated with the hospital charged the hospital's doctors and staff with "as they say, about a dozen cases on which to prefer charges—some serious, most of them utterly trivial—with the apparent intention of discrediting and thereby curtailing the usefulness of the institution or of degrading members of their own profession."

One such accusation involved the case of Homer Shirey. Dr. Guy Asper complained that Dr. Charles Palmer, who was affiliated with the hospital, had "stolen" his patient and then ignored advice from a specialist and botched the operation leading to Shirey's death. Palmer pointed out that nothing had been hidden from Asper, but Asper had refused to attend his patient as long as he was a patient of the Chambersburg Hospital.

Further, Shirey's brother submitted testimony that Palmer

hadn't tried to influence Homer to stay in Chambersburg Hospital. "I wish to say that it is with extreme regret I learn that there is (unreadable) one person in my native county of Franklin who is attacking an institution which has covered so many years of strenuous effort to secure. As a hospital, I deem the one at Chambersburg worthy of the praise of every citizen," A. E. Shirey wrote.

Palmer named not only Asper but Dr. J. E. Kempter as two of the leading opponents of the hospital. Because they weren't associated with the hospital, they couldn't get the same level of access to the hospital. They visited Palmer at one point and tried to get him to sign a petition to have all doctors allowed equal access to the hospital. Palmer told the committee, "and this request was fortified or weakened by an insult, a blackmailing threat, which set forth that if the directors did not open the doors, they would make public in various ways the knowledge of irregularities of the staff and nurses and directors."

In another instance, Drs. Brough and Kempter tracked down a former hospital patient, Mary Faubel, and in an "unfeeling and brusque" manner tried to get her to reshape her experience at the hospital so that it reflected negatively.

Faubel said that Brough had asked her to stop by his office and she did. "I went in and then he pushed the door shut and then sat down against the door and he was awful nervous and he frightened me. I never saw him look like that." He peppered Faubel with questions and criticized the work done at the hospital, trying to get Faubel to also criticize Palmer's work.

Brough also complained at length about the fact that Faubel had made a partial payment for her surgery. It made Faubel very uncomfortable because she said she had done nothing wrong.

When the unassociated doctors used the hospital, they complained about the nursing staff. The cause of the problem usually came down to the doctor trying to have the nurses do things that hospital policies forbid them from doing.

The Franklin County Medical Society tried to use the controversy to get the hospital to enact an open door policy in order to keep the society from preferring any charges against the hospital staff. It would have also ceded control of the hospital over to the medical society.

The investigation noted that giving into the demands "would involve the absolute surrender by the Board of Directors of the authority and right to appoint the staff of an institution which they now control as trustees of those who built and own it and to whom and to the patients committed to their care." The report noted that the public had built the hospital and should retain control, whereas the medical society had contributed only a tiny fraction.

The problem was not the hospital but the medical society. "On the contrary, the attitude of the members of the Franklin County Medical Society seemed from the first to be either that of indifference or open hostility. The report noted that the medical society hadn't been that supportive of the hospital. For example, the Lincoln East Way building had cost $18,000 to build, which was raised through donations from the community, but the medical society donated only $100.

With the public airing of this dispute, the rift caused by misunderstandings was put aside and eventually the hospital and medical society staff and doctors were able to forge a good working relationship.

At Mont Alto, the Patients Ran the Hospital

For people who suddenly felt they had no control over their lives or their futures, the Mont Alto Sanitorium gave them some of that control back.

The Mont Alto Sanitorium first opened in Mont Alto and Pennsylvania in 1901 as a single, small building called White Haven on South Mountain where it was believed the fresh air of the higher elevations would help people recover their health. Elwell Stockdale was the medical director.

The facility grew, but the buildings were unheated barns and tents. Private donations allowed small cabins to be built in 1902. The cabins were 8x10-feet large and housed five people.

As the need for the facility's services grew, the Pennsylvania state legislature finally invested in the property so that durable buildings could be constructed for the thirty patients. An office building, spring house, six three-room cottages, and an assembly building costing $8,000 were built in 1903.

Each of the patients paid $1 a week to stay at the sanitorium hoping to gain relief from diseases such as tuberculosis. The payment covered all the expenses except laundry. There were also no medical costs involved since there was no medical doctor on site.

In 1907, the Pennsylvania Department of Health took over the facility and spent $600,000 improving it.

The sanitorium finally got an infirmary in 1910 and by

1912, 960 patients were staying at Mont Alto. While the patients lived in larger cottages and things had improved, there were still problems. For instance, patient mail was often marked "contaminated" at the post office and discarded. This led to the sanitorium getting its own post office in 1915.

By this time, Dr. R. H. McCutcheon had become the medical director. He decided in 1924 that it would help his patients if they felt they had a little more control over their lives.

The infirmary at the Mont Alto Sanitorioum. Courtesy of Wikimedia Commons.

When a new community hall had opened, the patients appointed a committee of ushers to maintain order in the hall. The idea worked so well that McCutcheon decided to allow the patients to govern themselves.

"These tuberculosis victims, drawn from every walk of life, today virtually run the large state reservation to which they hastened in the effort to restore the health sapped by long hours in an office or factory. Forced to leave their families and go to the sanitorium in a final effort to prolong their lives, they have thrust aside the pangs of homesickness and applied themselves wholeheartedly to the task of administering the affairs of their own community," the *Gettysburg Times* reported.

A postcard aerial view of the Mont Alto Sanitorium in the 1940s. Courtesy of Wikimedia Commons.

Every ambulatory patient was given a voice in the management of every detail of the sanitorium except for administrative issues. Once, a Philadelphia police officer and former prize fighter came to Mont Alto as a patient. He had a temper and tried to assault an usher. The man was taken before the committee, who listened to his explanation of the event and that of the usher's before recommending that the man be expelled from the sanitorium. McCutcheon approved the recommendation, and the angry man was sent home.

The patients met once a month to vote on various issues and assign responsibilities to different patients.

No preference was given to what the patient might have

done before coming to the sanitorium. Thomas Noonan, a former clerk, was voted in as the unofficial mayor.

The result was that the mood around the facility quickly improved as the patients took pride in managing their lives. A reception committee was formed to welcome new patients and introduce them to Mont Alto's form of self-government. Things ran so well that McCutcheon didn't even need to attend the monthly meetings.

"Things are so different now from what they used to be. Before the people came here, looking forward to death only as a means of ending their suffering. Now they take an active interest in the camp and everybody is apparently benefitting. We sort of hate to leave now, even when we are cure," the *Gettysburg Times* quoted one patient as saying.

Later in 1924, Noonan was expected to leave the facility because his health had improved. He was going to return to Philadelphia and become a purser on a steamship. While he was reluctant to leave, he made plans to have the committee vote on whom the new mayor would be.

The site served as a sanatorium into the 1960s when it began to focus on geriatrics. Today, it is the home of the Cornel Abraxas Leadership Development Program, a program designed to help troubled adolescent boys.

Paying the Rose Rent

Each year, congregations of three churches in Chambersburg offer a single rose to a member of the city's founding family. It is a simple gift, but one that has been given year after year, decade after decade, century after century without fail.

The reason the rose is given each year is simple. The rent must be paid.

Benjamin Chambers founded Chambersburg in 1734 when a representative of the Penn family issued him a "Blunston license" for 400 acres. Because of the area's Scotch and Irish residents, the Falling Spring Presbyterian Church was the first church established in the town. In 1768, Chambers gave the congregation land for a church and cemetery in 1768 because he recognized the role that religion played in creating a community and giving it a moral core.

In 1780, he offered land to the First Lutheran Church and Zion Reformed Church, which were both working to grow and establish themselves in the town. All that he asked in return for the land was that an annual rent of a single red rose be paid to his family or a descendant.

"One of the stipulations in the deed is that it had to be a rose from the church's grounds," said Rev. Jeffrey Diller of the Zion Reformed Church.

It is not known why Chambers chose such an unusual rent payment, but the red rose has some biblical connections.

Early Christians said that the five petals of a red rose are symbolic of the five wounds of Jesus Christ. The color is also associated with the blood of Christian martyrs or representative of the Virgin Mary. Some legends say that white roses grew in the Garden of Eden, but they turned red with shame when Adam and Eve fell from grace.

One of these may have been Chambers' reason for choosing the red rose as payment, or it may simply have been his favorite flower.

"The son, Capt. Benjamin had roses lining his walk in front of his house which would have been part of the original settlement of the founder. Later, the area became known as Rosedale," said Ann Hull, executive director of the Franklin County Historical Society.

Diller also noted that it may have simply been fashionable at the time to give churches land that way. He said that he knows of many other churches throughout the region that pay a similar annual rent.

Whatever the reason, his foresight and generosity allowed the churches to establish themselves in the town.

"We make a big thing of it each year with a program that celebrates the historical aspect of the ceremony," Diller said.

During a different Sunday in June, each church has a special service in which a member of the Chambers family is presented with the rose rent.

The Zion Reformed Church service begins with a fellowship breakfast on the morning of the second Sunday in June. This is followed by a historical presentation to place the event in context, the ceremony to select the rose and the celebration of the presentation of the rose rent.

Since 2007, Franklin County has also paid another rose rent. It is based on a deed that the late John George, a descendant of the founding Chambers family, found in the Franklin County Courthouse. The 1785 deed transferred lots to the county to hold a courthouse and jail in exchange for a rose rent.

Franklin County Commissioner G. Warren Elliot made the first payment of the rent to George's widow, June, in July 2007, when he gave her a dozen roses.

The payment of the rose rent at the Zion Reformed Church in Chambersburg, Pennsylvania. Courtesy of the Zion Reformed Church.

Building an Educational System in Franklin County

The Chambersburg School District has about 8,800 pupils nowadays, but when public education came to Franklin County in 1834, there were only 337 students in the district.

And forget the little brick or clapboard one-room school house. Franklin County's earliest schools were log cabins, and students were lucky to have that. The 1834 school budget was $426.24, and the school system had no authority to levy taxes for additional revenues.

"With its rude logs, puncheon floor, slab benches, open-throated chimney, it served as a people's college to prepare boys and girls to become the future men and women of the neighborhood, the citizens of the commonwealth," Samuel Bates wrote in *History of Franklin County* in 1887.

Free public education came to Franklin County within five months after the Commonwealth of Pennsylvania approved a free public school system in the state, according to the *Public Opinion*.

It didn't matter so much how things were taught in those days, but what was taught. If a classroom even had textbooks, they were basic ones, such as a spelling book, grammar book, an English reader, a United States history book, a basic math book, and even the Bible.

"Slates and black-boards were, at first, unknown; and steel pens likewise. The ever-faithful goose quill, made and sharpened by the master's skillful knife, supplied the penmanship of the times," Bates wrote.

These early school houses were basically furnished. It was more essential that the students have desks and chairs than some of the fancier things found in later classrooms.

"No globes or wall maps, no numeral frames or other objects of illustration, cumbered the humble log schoolhouse. Work was done in a humble manner, and good work too. Pupils learned because they appreciated their opportunities," Bates wrote.

The teachers from those days didn't have college degrees in education. They were learned men and women who had an interest in teaching children. Even fifty years later, Bates could still remember his teachers, including one named Daniel Eckerman.

Bates said Eckerman was "an excellent instructor, who wrote a hand like copper plate; spelled correctly; whose pronunciation was faultless and distinct; a good arithmetician; understood grammar and geography, and wouldn't lick me, because I had spoken truthfully when I had gotten into a little scrape. His kindly admonition is by no means forgotten, though it was given fifty-two years ago. The lesson was a valuable one."

Another teacher he remembered was Captain Isaac Miller. Miller was both Bates' teacher and, later, a fellow teacher later. Miller taught in Chambersburg for around half a century, according to Bates.

"Who didn't know him? A good penman, and the very man who could manage schools with a hard reputation. He had an abiding faith in a liberal application of Solomon's celebrated cure for a fool's back, and at the same time could work out any number of knotty problems. As he taught many years, ho was also contemporaneous as a teacher during my career," Bates wrote.

Despite Miller's long-serving career, other teachers didn't last nearly as long.

"Why are they no longer teaching here? The case is plain enough. School directors are generally selected because they pay a good deal of school tax, or such as are in favor of low taxes for school purposes, and such as favor low salaries and short schoolterms. The natural consequences have followed. Salaries from $20 to per month for five or six months are not exactly calculated to keep in the ranks, or in the district, teachers with professional papers," Bates wrote.

From these modest beginnings, the Chambersburg School District grew into the $160.4 million school system that it is today.

County Gets a Vo-Tech School

Though the Franklin County Career and Technical Center cost a lot more to build, served a much smaller community, and took longer to build than originally imagined, the result was a vocational and technical school that has graduated thousands of skilled workers over its forty-one years. Not only that, but ninety-eight percent of them have been able to remain in the area after graduation because they had the skills that local employers needed.

The idea of a vocational-technical school for Franklin County was first suggested as part of a statewide plan for such schools. At that time, it was envisioned that one school could serve students in Franklin, Adams, Fulton and part of Cumberland counties.

The idea was kicked around for a couple of years until a group of people from the business, agricultural and education communities formed in 1963 to look at how to make the idea a reality. Gradually, the school's district shrunk until it became Franklin County and the Shippensburg area of Cumberland County.

Industries and businesses in the proposed area were sent 1,680 surveys to determine what skills students needed to have to be employable and what business areas were most in need of workers. About eighty percent of the surveys were returned, and that information, along with the results of a student interest survey, were reviewed by the committee to come up with twenty-two proposed courses of study.

The proposed school was presented to the school boards

in twenty-three different school districts in two counties for their review. In March 1964, 108 directors from those boards met in a special meeting to decide on whether building a new vo-tech school was a workable idea.

Clair Fitz, area coordinator of industrial education at Penn State, spoke to the directors about the opportunities a vo-tech school would present. "Saying vocational-technical schools provide sound terminal education for those pupils not planning to continue into college, Fitz added that skills learned in these schools give pupils 'something to sell' when they enter the labor market following completion of their schooling. The new skills; he continued, will give the county a better and higher labor market and generally bolster the county's economy," reported *The Public Opinion*.

After two hours of discussion, the vote was unanimous to submit an application for a new school to the state. George Fries, who was a member of the committee, called the vote, "a fine, progressive step forward."

At this point, it was believed that the school could open in 1966 at the latest and cost $1.2 million to build. The Pennsylvania Department of Education gave the project its go ahead, and the search began for a site where the school could be built.

Eventually 108 acres were purchased in Guilford Springs, but construction issues, including how to get adequate water to the site, delayed the project and increased the costs. Construction began mid-1968.

The school partially opened in the fall of 1969 with fourteen areas of study. Another seven areas were added the next semester. The total cost of construction came in at $4.2 million.

"That $4.2 million will pay for a sprawling modern building that features the latest in automotive repair shops, a practical nursing suite, and even a temperature controlled hothouse for agriculture students," reported *The Public Opinion*.

Initial enrollment in the school was 227 students from the six participating school districts of Chambersburg, Fannett-Metal, Greencastle-Antrim, Shippensburg, Tuscarora and Waynesboro. The students attended the vo-tech center for three weeks to train in their skill areas and then their home schools for three weeks to complete their general educational requirements.

The Franklin County Area Vocational-Technical School as it appeared during the dedication in 1970. Scanned from the dedication ceremony program.

The Franklin County Area Vocational-Technical School was formally dedicated on April 19, 1970. In his dedicatory remarks, Superintendent James Gibboney said, "A vocational-technical education will help our youth to cultivate the ability to construct their own environment and to create their own destiny. Through your united efforts you have placed a monument here. Not a monument of brick and stone and steel, but a monument to the living, to the minds of men."

Though the name has changed to the Franklin County Career and Technology Center, the school still remains a monument that grows and adapts to provide the county with a skilled labor force.

A Chambersburg Supermarket that was Ahead of Its Time

William Ensminger and H. M. Carl founded City Produce Company in 1925 when chain grocery stores like A&P and Kroger began seeing growth. The two men worked hard to grow their business and in 1943 Carl and his wife, Lula, took over the store and renamed it Carl's Market. They also expanded the produce and fruit company into a full-service market.

The couple worked hard, serving their customers, growing their business, and learning what customers wanted. The Carls started their own supermarket chain when they opened a second market in 1955 in Waynesboro. However, it wasn't until the following year they were able to open their ultimate vision of a supermarket, which, in many ways, is still unmatched today.

The third Carl's Market opened as the anchor store in the new Town and Country Shopping Center on Lincoln Highway in July 1956. It was the third-largest supermarket in Pennsylvania, both in floor space and merchandise stock, according to the *Public Opinion*. The store had about 20,000 square feet of space with 12,000 square feet of that dedicated to selling space. Out front, the shopping center had parking for 300 cars.

Grocery stores had been evolving for years, bringing in new departments so customers didn't have to go to a grocer, farmer's market, and butcher shop to get all their food needs.

"In 1930, Michael Cullen, a former executive of both Kroger and A&P, opened his first King Kullen store, widely cited as America's first supermarket, although others have some legitimate claim to that title as well," according to *Groceteria.com*.

By the time the Carls opened their second market, the concept of supermarkets had largely taken hold. It was aided by the growth of American suburbs that also allowed for the building of larger stores. Carl's Market took the concept of a supermarket a leap forward, though.

Customers entered and left the air-conditioned store through "Magic Carpet doors." These automatic doors are quite common at stores today, but they were a new, innovative feature at stores in 1956.

Carl's Market had more than fifty employees working in dozens of different departments, including a courtesy counter where customers could cash checks. The store's key personnel were Product Manager Al Jones, Meat Department Manager William Renfrew and Grocery Manager James Fahnestock.

"The gourmet's department is stocked with hundreds of items from many parts of the world: fried grasshoppers, rattlesnake meat, quail eggs, bean and bamboo shoots, together with the more conventional items," the *Public Opinion* reported.

Another of the new departments was called the "Green Thumb Corner" where customers could purchase garden supplies and flower arrangements.

A unique feature unseen in grocery stores today was a customer lounge. Mothers could shop while children relaxed in the lounge and watched television. In other areas of the store customers could find an automatic orange juicing machine to get fresh-squeezed juice and a hickory smoke barbeque pit.

"Among the other, less conventional departments will be those offering special diet foods, household items, paper products and stationery, health and beauty aids, and magazines," the newspaper reported.

Another family owned supermarket chain, Weis Markets, bought Carl's Markets in 1965. The location for the Lincoln Highway Carl's Market is now the location of Super Shoes on Lincoln Way East.

BEHIND BARS

Jailbreak! Not!

The men had worked patiently under the cover of darkness, scraping at mortar and wiggling bricks until they could pull the bricks free from the wall. Gaitano D'Anna and Raymond A. Chapelle then carefully stacked the bricks in the darkest corner of their cell and flushed the dirt and mortar down the toilet.

They must have realized their problem after the first few bricks were removed, but the two New Yorkers were determined to get out of the Franklin County Jail in December 1949. The jail designers had other ideas, though. It had been built to replace a jail with poorly constructed walls. It had even survived the burning of Chambersburg by Confederate soldiers in 1864.

D'Anna and Chapelle didn't realize this. All they knew was that "A steel plate, inserted between the outer and inner brick walls of the jail building, prevented the two men from boring the hole to the outside," according to the *Public Opinion.*

Their cell was on the first floor of the western cell block of the jail. The two men, plus a third companion Louis A. Schipani, who was in another cell, had pleaded guilty to burglary a month earlier. Sentenced to prison, the men had no intention of serving out their time. They had concocted their escape plan by breaking off a two-foot section of one of the iron beds in the cell. This was their tool to scrape at the mortar and pry the bricks free.

When the men heard movement in the hallway, they would stop their work and cover the bricks in the corner and the hole in the wall with paper.

However, on Saturday evening, Dec. 3, the footsteps in the hall stopped outside their cell and the door opened. Sheriff Robert I. Oliver stood there with a deputy. Oliver stepped into the cell and removed the paper cover the hole in the wall. The escape plan had been discovered when another prisoner leaked the scheme to the prison warden.

The Franklin County Jail when it was still in operation in the mid-20th century. Courtesy of the Franklin County Historical Society – Kittochtinny.

Not that the men would have gotten far. Even if there had been no steel plate to keep them in their cell, the newspaper noted that "Had the youths reached the outside, they would have found themselves inside the enclosed jail yard and would have been faced with the problem of scaling the 30-foot stone wall."

The sheriff removed the two prisoners from the compromised cell and place them in another one which undoubtedly had a sturdier bed.

News of the breakout attempt leaked out Tuesday morning when the sheriff asked the county commissioners to authorize repair work for the damaged cell.

What is now called the Old Jail when it was built to replace the county's first official jail in 1818. It is the oldest jail building in Pennsylvania, though it is now home to the Franklin County Historical Society. It was used as a jail until 1971 and had the longest continuous use of any jail in the state. At times, it was also home to the county sheriff.

The Downtown Chambersburg website notes that "According to local legend, the basement dungeons of the jail were used as a stop on the Underground Railroad during the Civil War."

Franklin County's Last Hanging

The crime

On April 30, 1912, William Reed was executed for a murder he never denied committing.

The forty-two-year-old Reed had a reputation as an honest and hard laborer. More importantly, he didn't have a record as a troublemaker, but on May 9, 1911, he had been drinking on and off for a couple of days and had finally come to decision. He took the train from Waynesboro, Pennsylvania, to Mont Alto, Pennsylvania.

The Pennsylvania State Forest Academy in Mont Alto was one of the first forestry schools in the country, established by the governor of Pennsylvania in 1903. Today, it is Penn State's Mont Alto Campus.

Reed had worked at the academy for a short time in 1907, and it was there that he met Sarah (Sadie) Hurley Mathna. She was a single mother whose husband had abandoned her, leaving her struggling to get by. She couldn't even afford to raise her daughter Della. The eight-year-old was living with friends of Mathna's in Guilford.

Reed and Mathna had taken a liking to each other and moved in together for about a year between 1908 and 1909. They split up when Mathna moved to Chambersburg to work in the Miller Hotel, while Reed worked as a laborer for different businesses in Waynesboro. They still saw each other on weekends, but they began drifting apart, or at least, Mathna began considering ending the relationship.

She eventually returned to Forest Academy to work in the

kitchen, and it was there that Reed found her on May 9. By the time he arrived, breakfast was finished, and there was no one else in the kitchen except for Mathna, who was grinding coffee.

What was said between the two of them is not known. Only Reed was around later to give his version, which was that he asked Mathna for some papers and pictures there were his. She gave him some of them, but she told Reed that she had burned the rest of the papers and pictures. This is what Reed said enraged him.

He drew his .38 caliber revolver and fired three shots, hitting Sarah in the neck, the cheek, and the chest. It would later be found that the last bullet pierced her heart and was the fatal shot.

The academy matron, Sarah Conklin, came running from the garden when she heard the shots. Another woman who helped in the kitchen, Margaret Brickers, was at the road buying bread from a baker's wagon when she heard the shots.

George Miley, the baker who was selling the bread to Brickers, saw Reed shoving a revolver in his pocket as he came out of the kitchen.

"I have just shot Sadie and have done for her," Reed told Miley.

Inside the building, Mathna had staggered out of the kitchen and collapsed on the floor in the dining room.

The group that found her there carried her upstairs to a lounge. She said nothing but "gave several gasps and died," according to the *Public Opinion*.

Reed just kept walking toward Mont Alto. Along the way, the wife of a doctor in Mont Alto approached him.

"Passing Mrs. Brosius at the latter's [house] she asked what was wrong at the Forestry School and he replied in a laughing way, easy in manner and very cool, 'My girl is sick' and passed on,'" reported the *Public Opinion*. Reed would deny saying this during the trial.

Pennsylvania State Forest Academy at Mont Alto. Courtesy of Wikimedia Commons.

He found his friend Romaine Small in town and told him, "Well, she's dead! I've shot Sadie and I'm going to give myself up!" Then Reed walked to the Constable Jacob Wile's office. He explained what had happened and surrendered.

Throughout all the events following the shooting, Reed appeared "perfectly cool and calm," according to the newspaper.

While sitting in county jail awaiting trial, the *Public Opinion* interviewed Reed. He said, "I didn't go there to kill here. I went there to get some of my letters and pictures. We had some words. I pulled out my revolver and began firing to scare her. The shooting of the revolver was no accident. I don't know why I shot her. I lost my head. You know how it is when you get mad."

Following the coroner's inquest, Mathna's body was taken to Roxbury. Services were held in the United Brethren Church, and she was buried there.

The punishment

William Reed had shot and killed Sarah Mathna on May 9, 1911. That was not in doubt. Even Reed admitted it. However, the real question that the Franklin County jury had to determine was whether Reed had gone to the State Forestry Academy in Mont Alto intending to kill Mathna or whether he had temporarily lost his senses when he killed her.

Attorneys J.W. Hoke and Irvin C. Elder began laying out their case to save Reed's life on September 7, 1911. They were opposed by District Attorney D. Edward Long who told the jury that Reed had committed premeditated murder. After three days of testimony, the jury retired at 4:42 p.m. on a Saturday and returned a verdict of guilty of murder on Sunday at 7 p.m. The difficulty in reaching a decision can be seen in the fact that it took 14 ballots to reach a decision.

Reed was sentenced to be hanged by the neck until dead.

Under state law, death sentences were automatically appealed at the state level. Reed was kept in the women's quarters of the county jail during this time so that he was separate from the other prisoners. His cell was on the second floor on the west side. The sheriff also set a death watch on him while he awaited his appeal.

During his months-long wait in the jail, passersby got used to seeing Reed's face in the second-floor window. The school children took to calling it "Reed's Window," according to the *Public Opinion*.

When Reed's appeal failed to overturn his death sentence, his execution was scheduled.

"On the day before his death, it is said he called out the

window to some boys something to the effect that he was to be hanged the next day, but had one more day to live. He held up one finger to at least one man who passed, indicating that but one more day on earth was left to him," the *Public Opinion* reported.

If this troubled Reed, he didn't show it. He slept well the night of April 29.

On Tuesday morning, April 30, "The day was gloomy, rain drizzling, it was cold and penetrating and added to the depression of the little band assembled inside the canvas enclosure waiting for the most dreadful sight in human possibilities to witness," according to the newspaper.

Reed had no special request for his last meal. He dressed himself in a black suit with a striped white shirt and "blue four-in-hand tie and low collar."

Before the appointed hour, he accepted a visit from Rev. W. C. Cremer. The clergyman held a special service in Reed's cell that morning.

As Reed was led from his cell, his last words were, "I thank all my friends and everybody who has expressed sympathy for me. I am sorry for my deed. I forgive everybody and hope all will forgive me for anything I may have done to others."

Outside the jail, crowds had been forming on King and Second streets to see the first hanging in Franklin County in thirty-three years. "Points of vantage on trees, poles and roofs near the jail had men and boys perched thereon," the newspaper reported. The police tried to keep the crowd moving, but they simply circled the block and returned. Children who were in the school next door were kept inside and away from the windows.

Reed appeared at the back of the jail at 10 a.m. with Sheriff George Walker and Deputy Ellsworth W. Kuhn. They walked across a gangway from the back porch of the jail to the gallows. Even facing death, Reed appeared calm as he glanced down at the fifty or so people who had been allowed into the courtyard to witness the execution.

The old gallows at the Franklin County Jail. Courtesy of the Franklin County Historical Society – Kittochtinny.

He walked steadily "as if promenading the streets," the newspaper reported. He stopped on the trapdoor.

The sheriff placed the noose around Reed's neck and then a black cloth bag over his head. Walker pulled the knot tight behind Reed's left ear and Reed grunted as if it had hurt him. Kuhn bound Reed's ankles together while Walker cuffed Reed's hands behind his back.

Walker stepped back to the lever, glanced at Kuhn, and pulled it at 10:06 a.m. The trapdoor fell open and Reed dropped about six feet. It was reported that he had no pulse about a minute later, though his heart continued beating. Dr. J. H. Devor and Coroner J. P. Macay pronounced Reed dead at 10:16 a.m.

"If it is the right idea to instill in human minds a fear to commit murder by making the law's vengeance horrible and fearsome through capital punishment, then it seems to us that hanging is the way to effect the purpose. Staring with eyes wavering through innate repulsion at that instrument of death which by right takes equal rank with those of the inquisition one could not well conjure a punishment more debasing or more to be dreaded by man," the *Public Opinion* reported.

Reed's body was taken by train to Mont Alto later that day and the last person to be hanged in the county was interred beside his parents.

Franklin County Jail Hosts Its First Wedding

Franklin County has had a jail since 1797, although it was first authorized three years prior. Over the years, thousands of prisoners were kept in the cells of the Franklin County Jail in Chambersburg, Pennsylvania, but only once has a couple been married there.

In 1969, Thurman Gelwicks and Arlene Bateman were growing excited as their wedding date approached. They had planned on being married on Oct. 20 in the office of Justice of the Peace Mabel Bateman, but an hour before their wedding, police arrested Gelwicks on a non-support charge. He had accumulated $1,921 in unpaid support for his former wife and seven children.

Gelwicks was imprisoned in the second Franklin County Jail, which was built in 1818. It is a two-story building with a slate roof and cupola. At the time, the building was over 150 years old and not in the best shape.

Things were looking bad for Gelwicks and Bateman as far as their nuptials went. They talked about their situation and decided that they still wanted to get married.

"The new Mrs. Gelwicks said their marital permit was only good for 60 days, and Gelwicks is serving a sentence of up to four months. Since she had already requested a three-day leave from her work at Stanley Manufacturing Co., the couple thought they might as well go ahead with the ceremony... no matter where," Jayne S. Thomas wrote in the *Public*

Opinion.

Shoemaker and Bateman met Gelwicks in a "bleak, drafty office" on Oct. 22. Gelwicks, who was described as a short, stocky man, wore a plaid shirt. Bateman "chose a long-sleeved royal blue bonded knit dress with attractive multi-colored scarf," Thomas wrote.

The old Franklin County Jail when it still operated. Courtesy of the Franklin County Historical Society – Kittochtinny.

"A handful of men and women witnessed the brief ceremony in the office of the jail. There were no floral bouquets, just a huge calendar and coats hanging on the walls. Heavy grey desks and black lacquered chairs replaced wooden pews," the Public Opinion reported.

Bateman was a bit shy and nervous as she recited her wedding vows, and she stumbled over them. No rings were exchanged during the ceremony.

"They won't be in until the end of the week," Bateman explained.

Despite the missteps, Thomas said that the ceremony was a touching one.

After the ceremony, the new Mrs. Gelwicks returned to her home in Fayetteville and her job at the Stanley Manufacturing Co. She scrimped and saved and was able to pay $500 towards her husband's back support in early December. This good-faith effort satisfied the courts.

"Thurman Gelwicks was free to go on a honeymoon Wednesday, 42 days after he married Arlene Bateman in the Franklin County Jail," the *Hagerstown Daily Mail* reported on Dec. 4.

He had served about six weeks of his sentence, but he was also required as a condition of his release to pay $77 a week for support of his former wife, Pauline Gelwicks, and their seven children. He also had to pay an additional $10 a week to pay off his remaining unpaid support.

The old Franklin County Jail was placed on the National Register of Historic Places the following year. The building is now home to the Franklin County Historical Society – Kittochtinny's museum and genealogy library.

It also served as an appropriate wedding chapel. When Gelwicks died in 1983, he and Arlene were still married.

Disease & Disaster

Infant Paralysis Hits the County

At first, parents thought their children had been playing too hard. They developed fevers and some of them got headaches. The symptoms would pass, though, but then a few days later, the children would get stiff necks or backs. Some would experience constipation. If they were lucky, that is all that would happen.

Unfortunately, not all the children were lucky. Some of them would be playing and fall over, unable to use their legs or arms. Others would wake up in the morning, unable to move. A few even died, unable to breathe.

The disease was called infant paralysis in 1918, though it is now better known as polio. The epidemic in Franklin County began in Waynesboro in June 1918 and continued through the fall. Forty-six cases were reported in the county with six children dying because of the disease. Chambersburg had fifteen of those cases and two deaths.

Though polio has been around for centuries, major epidemics weren't seen until the early 20th century when they appeared in Europe and the United States.

Polio damages the nerve cells, which affect a person's muscle control. Without nerve stimulation, the muscles weaken and atrophy. This can lead to paralysis, and if the muscles that help the body breathe are affected, the paralysis can cause death because a patient cannot breathe.

Two years prior to the Franklin County epidemic, there had been over 27,000 cases of polio in the United States, resulting in over 6,000 deaths.

The first line of defense in fighting polio was to quarantine homes where there were outbreaks of polio, and the families had to place placards in their windows as a notice of the quarantine.

Sometimes it would go further. An infant girl of the H. H. Harrison family in Guilford Township was stricken with polio in September 1918. Though she was not in serious condition, "She has eight brothers and sisters all at home and all attending school in Guilford. The school will be ordered closed today by Health Officer Kinter. The home will be will be quarantined today," the *Chambersburg Public Opinion* reported.

ANTERIOR POLIOMYELITIS!
INFANTILE PARALYSIS

"Act of Assembly approved May 14, 1909, provides that anyone violating the provisions of this Act, upon conviction thereof may be sentenced to pay a fine of not less than $10.00 or more than $100.00, to be paid to the use of said county, or to be imprisoned in the county jail for a period of not less than ten days or more than thirty days, or both, at the discretion of the court."

BY ORDER OF THE BOARD OF HEALTH.

Health Officer.

Address.

A board of health polio quarantine order. Courtesy of Wikimedia Commons.

Sanitary and hygiene campaigns were undertaken to encourage people to drink and bathe in clean water. Better hygiene meant that not only was it less likely a child, or even an adult would develop polio, but also more likely that the symptoms would be mild. However, this also meant that it was more likely that older children would develop polio and it would be the harsher, paralyzing form.

Little more could be done because doctors of the time were uncertain just what polio was, and it was decades before a vaccine would be developed.

A 1916 article in the *New York Times* outlined the problem that doctors faced, noting "fighting infantile paralysis consists largely in doing everything that seems effective in the hope that some of the measures taken will be effective."

Tony Gould wrote in *A Summer Plague: Polio and Its Survivors* about some of the treatments used at the time to unsuccessfully cure polio. Doctors would "Give oxygen through the lower extremities, by positive electricity. Frequent baths using almond meal, or oxidising the water. Applications of poultices of Roman chamomile, slippery elm, arnica, mustard, cantharis, amygdalae dulcis oil, and of special merit, spikenard oil and Xanthoxolinum. Internally use caffeine, Fl. Kola, dry muriate of quinine, elixir of cinchone, radium water, chloride of gold, liquor calcis and wine of pepsin."

Unfortunately for Franklin County, residents had just begun to breathe a sigh of relief from the infantile paralysis epidemic before they had to deal with an even greater threat called the Spanish Flu.

Don't Let the Flu Get You

In 1918, the world was at war. There was even an army camp in nearby Gettysburg, Pennsylvania, that helped prepare young men to become soldiers who could fight the Germans in World War I. They trained to fight the enemy using a piece of state-of-the-art military technology called the tank. However, the real enemy moved indiscriminately through camps and communities, injuring and killing men, women, soldier, children. It made no difference.

This war waged for about a year until the enemy retreated and hid, but not before killing an estimated sixty million people or more than four times the population of this state.

It was not World War I that killed all those people. It was the Spanish Flu. It was called Spanish Flu because it apparently first appeared in Spain, but it was simply that year's flu strain. And when it first appeared in the U.S. in the spring of 1918, it was a fairly typical flu. It was highly contagious, but it wasn't any more deadly than a typical flu strain. The problem with the flu virus is that it mutates, and some of those mutations can become deadly.

Imagine the terror people felt about a flu that killed sixty million people when the world's population was less than 1.9 billion. Two to three people out of every 100 across the world died. If the Spanish Flu struck today, the lethality would be around 180 million.

The Spanish Flu killed more people than World War I and in a shorter time frame, too, yet the war dominated the headlines during 1918 because it was winding down at the same time the Spanish Flu was reaching its peak. It was estimated that 675,000 Americans died from the Spanish Flu or ten times more than died in the war.

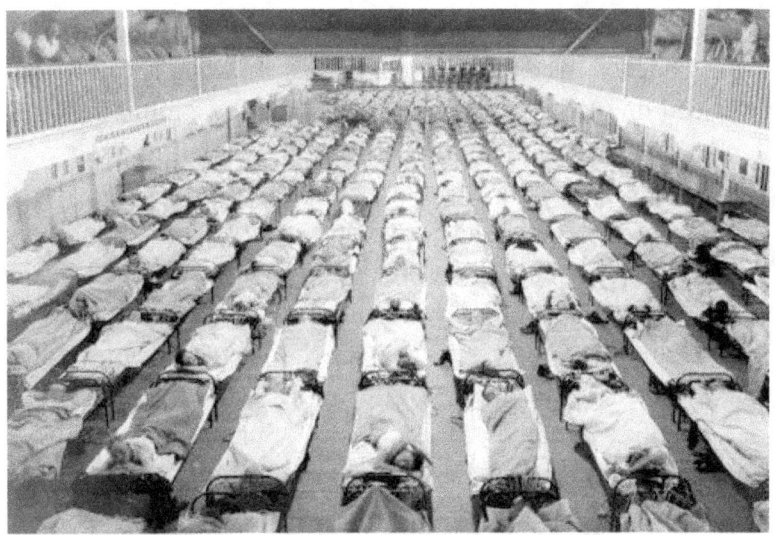

An emergency hospital for Spanish Flu patients in Kansas. Courtesy of Wikimedia Commons.

It killed more people in one year than the Black Plague did in four years.

It was so devastating that human life span was reduced by ten years in 1918.

One physician wrote that patients rapidly "develop the most vicious type of pneumonia that has ever been seen," and later, when cyanosis appeared in patients, "it is simply a struggle for air until they suffocate." Another doctor said that the influenza patients "died struggling to clear their airways of a blood-tinged froth that sometimes gushed from their mouth and nose."

Spanish Flu first appeared in Franklin County around the end of September 1918. The first death in the county from

Spanish Flu was a young girl who died of pneumonia on September 27. Spanish Flu was so under the radar at the time that no one even connected the death to Spanish Flu until after the danger had passed.

Nearly everyone saw no threat from the flu, and so, they were shocked when the *Chambersburg Public Opinion* announced on Oct. 4 that Acting State Health Commissioner B. F. Royer had issued "the most drastic quarantine order ever given in Pennsylvania" the day before. The order closed every moving picture house, every theater, every saloon and every place of public amusement, including pool rooms and dance halls. The sick couldn't have visitors unless they were so desperately ill that they weren't expected to live. And any visitors had to wear a gauze mask. All funerals had to be private.

Whether churches, schools, and Sunday schools were closed was left up to local boards of health. The Franklin County Board of Health voted to do so on Oct. 4. The *Public Opinion* noted that this was the first time in the history of Chambersburg that no public gatherings were permitted.

The article noted that 60,000 people in the Philadelphia area were already sick with the flu. Locally, Wilson College had forty cases of the flu or roughly twenty percent of its student body were sick. Camp Colt had had twenty-one deaths on Oct. 2, bringing the total deaths there to sixty-two. All of Dickinson College in Carlisle, Pennsylvania, was placed under quarantine on Oct. 3.

Some headlines on the front page of the newspaper on Oct. 5 were: "Flu holds back army movement," "Official order that closed up things in state," "Surgeon general blue appeals to states for action," "Flu spreading in the county," "More pneumonia, fairs called off in state," "Public obeying rules," and "Delaware is closed tight."

Overnight, the flu had seemingly jumped from inconvenience to epidemic.

That first weekend after the order in effect, two people in Chambersburg died. The *Public Opinion* noted on Oct. 7 that one doctor had seen thirty-five cases of flu on Sunday evening and another doctor had seen over 100 patients on Saturday.

Dr. Harvey Bridgers was a doctor in Blue Ridge Summit from 1917 to 1952. He wrote about his experiences during the flu epidemic. His preferred treatment was to try to force the fluids out of the body in order to lower a patient's fever. He would prescribe medication to do this and then have a person stay closed up in a room while fighting the fever because he had also noted that the flu seemed to thrive in fresh air.

As he tried to visit all of his patients, he would rush into their home and hand them some of his capsules. Then he would tell them, "Take one of these every three hours and drink a glass of water every half hour! If you can't do that, don't bother me—too many people are sick." Then he would run out to his next patient.

By Oct. 9, only five days after the health order had been imposed, there were more than 200,000 cases of flu in the state and 1,300 cases in Chambersburg. The *Public Opinion* noted, "Waynesboro after having boldly asserted that all the cases there were only colds yesterday became alarmed at the rapid spread of the flue (sic) in that town." Also, the death toll at Camp Colt was up to ninety-two.

By Oct. 14, the *Public Opinion* noted that more than ten percent of Chambersburg's population was in bed with the flu. Stores were closing by 6:30 p.m., and anyone caught spitting was arrested. On this day alone, 240 new cases of the flu were reported in Chambersburg.

Vick's VapoRub hit its stride at this time as a treatment for flu patients. The flu pandemic increased sales from $900,000 annually to $2.9 million.

In many cities, people had to wear face masks to ride public transportation or enter public places. Courtesy of Wikimedia Commons.

Rumors abounded. Bayer, the German drug company, was inserting flu germs into their aspirin. When you took aspirin for a headache, you would catch the flu and die. A German sub had crept into Boston Harbor and released the germs like mustard gas.

Another funny rumor was that people said if you drank you would kill the flu germs inside you with the alcohol. More likely, just didn't care then if you got sick.

As the flu continued its rampage, an emergency hospital was opened after one doctor visited a rooming house on South 2nd Street in Chambersburg and found Henry Gelwiler sick in bed. He'd been there five days with little food because he was too weak to get out of bed and he had no chamber pot. The doctor got the man a nurse and then began pushing for a hospital where the seriously ill could be brought to conserve the limited nursing resources. The old Cumberland Valley Railroad Station on 3rd Street was used, and it quickly had to have large tents added onto it to accommodate the need.

Oddly enough, during this time, Chambersburg Hospital wouldn't accept any flu patients. It wasn't their choice. The state had ordered it hopefully to keep the flu from spreading to other patients. This doesn't mean that the hospital wasn't busy. It was seeing an average of thirty-six non-flu patients a day, which was above average for them.

Waynesboro wound up opening two emergency hospitals.

In late October, a medical train from Maryland came to Chambersburg to help treat patients.

Doctors were still getting overworked. One doctor had seen 130 patients on Oct. 16 and there were hundreds of new cases still being reported daily. The need was so great that the newspaper noted that at least two eye doctors in Chambersburg went back to general practice temporarily. Doctors were also assigned zones in which they would care for any of the sick. The theory behind this is that it would save them time from running back and forth across the city to treat patients.

"People died so quickly and in such unprecedented numbers that, in some areas, fire houses were used as places for the dead which were awaiting their turns for embalming and interment," Dr. Bridger wrote.

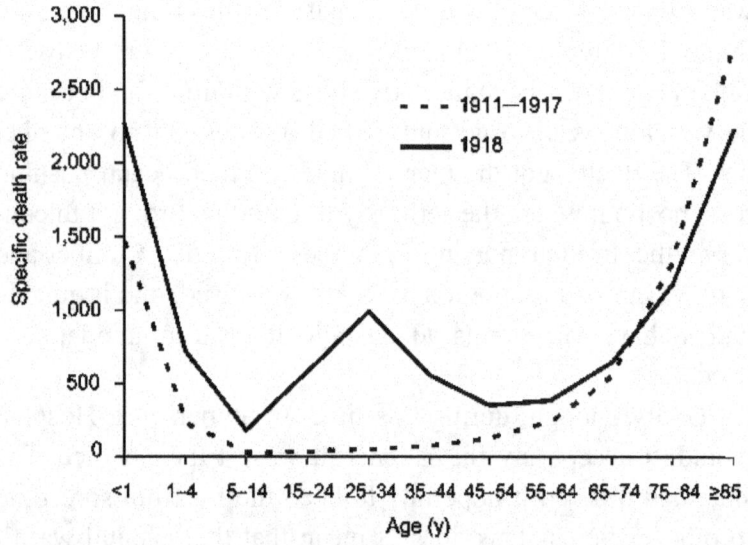

This chart shows the odd W-shaped mortality curve of Spanish Flu. Most diseases have a U-shaped mortality curve because the oldest and youngest in a population have the weakest immune systems.

And finally, a community kitchen was opened to provide meals to families in homes where everyone was sick in bed. By the time the crisis had passed, the kitchen had served 6,500 meals.

The *Public Opinion* reported on Oct. 20, "Yesterday, with rain coming down during all of the day, saw the streets almost depopulated. Doctors' automobiles, the motor messenger service and taxicabs were practically the only vehicles moving."

However, by this time, things had turned a corner. Illnesses were still high, but the numbers were coming down.

Startling stories also began emerging. On Oct. 22, a family of ten was found so sick that none of them had been out of bed in days. At the Scotland School, which stayed open, sixty percent of the students had the flu. At the United Brethren orphanage, there were fifty cases of the flu.

Halloween passed on Oct. 31 with no celebration.

The state finally lifted its ban on Nov. 9, and the local board of health quickly followed. The community kitchen and emergency hospitals closed as well.

This doesn't mean that everyone was suddenly fit and healthy. Battling the flu, wore people out, the *Public Opinion* noted, "For several weeks, it was a common sight on the streets to see convalescents creeping along, weak and lanquid, pale and enervated."

This is one of the insidious ways that the Spanish Flu worked. Many communities were already shorthanded medically because doctors had been drafted to serve in WWI. Then along came the flu, which intensified by the shortage by making many of the remaining doctors sick at a time when the workload was drastically increasing. The remaining doctors found themselves working longer hours with contagious people. This would wear them down and make them susceptible to flu and the process would repeat.

I talked about about Dr. Bridgers earlier. Well, he was one of those doctors whose overwork left him susceptible to the flu. Once he caught it, he stayed in bed. He still tried to write prescriptions for patients, but even that became too much for him.

By the time the flu abated in Chambersburg, the town had

had 3,000 cases or about twenty-three percent of the population. Although county numbers aren't available, it is estimated Franklin County probably had somewhere in the area of 14,260 cases of the flu in those couple months. Also, out of the 103 deaths during that time, 88 of them were from the flu. Extrapolating from that, there were probably about 420 flu deaths in the county. The *Public Opinion* noted that the death rate during that time was four time higher than average. The paper also noted that 108 children were made orphans or part orphans because of the flu.

The Great 1936 Flood

When it rains, it pours, as they say. And it rained a lot in March 1936. What's more is that the winter in many areas of the northeast and mid-Atlantic had seen a lot of snow over the winter. Because the temperatures had climbed above freezing what could have been more snow that March was rain. However, that rain pelted the snowpack on the mountains, melting it. The ground was still frozen mostly so all of that rain and melted snow had nowhere to go but downhill.

All over the northeast, water filled up the streams and rivers beyond their capacity, leading to one of the worst floods that the region has seen. While Franklin County wasn't on the receiving end of the worst flooding, it had problems.

The bridge to the CCC Camp at Old Forge was underwater and threatened to wash away downstream.

"Water was knee deep from the White Mill to the crossroads, and at points toward Waynesboro near the Middour Dam," Carl V. Besore and Robert L. Ringer wrote in *A Reflection of the History of Waynesboro, Pennsylvania and Vicinity.*

Fields were underwater if they were near a stream, and Cold Spring Park in Waynesboro was also underwater.

"The borough sewer project was underway at the time. Where it had been completed and backfilled in sub-freezing weather, it sank and made the streets impassable. Where it was still open, it filled with water, some of which found its way into cellars," Besore and Ringer wrote.

The rain apparently weakened the foundation of the S.D. Hockman building at Main and Potomac in Waynesboro, and it collapsed.

Mud also became a problem on the roads. According to *A Reflection of the History of Waynesboro, Pennsylvania and Vicinity*, ashes and gravel had been used on the roads for traction, but it turned to mud once it mixed with the floodwater.

The 1936 flood in Harrisburg was deep enough that people could row boats down the streets.

"Thirty or so seagulls landed in the Omar Frantz field adjacent to a branch of the Antietam. This was the first time gulls were ever sighted in Franklin County," Besore and Ringer wrote. "It was thought that they came from the Bay following the flooded area upstream, and then turned inland."

As bad as things got in Franklin County, at least no one died in the flooding. In the eleven states affected by the flooding, 178 people died from the March flood with about half of them being in Pennsylvania.

"Across the state more than 82,000 buildings (including 38,000 houses) were destroyed or damaged. Altogether,

242,698 people received Red Cross aid. The coal-producing and industrial cities of eastern Pennsylvania were flooded, as were many of the mines," according to the Sunbury Municipal Authority Flood Control report, *The Floods of 1936 and the Copeland Flood Control Bill.*

Property damage in Pennsylvania totaled $212.5 million ($3.5 billion in today's dollars).

Along the Potomac River, Hancock, Maryland, was under five feet of water by 2 a.m. on Mar. 12 with the river still rising at 1.5 feet an hour. The river peaked at 49.6 feet above normal at midnight on Mar. 18. At Williamsport, Md., this was six feet higher than it had been during the historic Johnstown Flood.

Rowboat traffic on community streets during the 1936 flood in Harrisburg.

A Pioneering Surgery Extends a Young Boy's Life

In the summer of 1949, Melvin "Brownie" McSherry, of Rouzerville, got sick. It wasn't an uncommon occurrence for a young teenager, but for Brownie, it was the beginning of something that would kill him.

"He couldn't keep food in his stomach and he had fits of coughing every night," the *Gettysburg Times* reported.

By October, the thirteen-year-old's weight was just forty-eight pounds and his parents, Melvin L. and Martha Green McSherry, admitted him to a hospital. They weren't a wealthy family who could afford to pay for an extended hospital stay, but an anonymous Waynesboro family picked up all the costs of the hospital stay.

Brownie's diagnosis was not good. He had cystic fibrosis, which is a recessive genetic disorder that affects the lungs, pancreas, liver and intestine with cysts. Dorothy Hansine Andersen first described the disease in 1938, two years after Brownie was born. Theories about cystic fibrosis changed throughout the 1940s as doctors learned more about it. At one point, it was believed to be related to a Vitamin A deficiency. During this time, antibiotics, especially penicillin, were used as a treatment, which is most likely what Brownie received while he was in the hospital the first time.

He returned home weighing seventy pounds in time to spend the holidays with his family, including his grandparents who lived in Gettysburg.

However, by January 1950, his condition took a turn for the worse, and he was admitted to Johns Hopkins Hospital in Baltimore to undergo "treatment which it is hoped will save, or at least prolong, his life. He is suffering from a rare disease which, unless checked, will cause his death, specialists say, in less than a year," the *Gettysburg Times* reported.

Though the newspaper reports were vague on what the treatment involved, it was apparently an operation to remove some cysts from his lungs. A specialist from New Orleans had successfully performed a similar operation once before on a patient and it was deemed successful.

"The doctor was contacted and it is hoped that his advice will be the one chance that will save Brownie's life," the newspaper reported.

Brownie's spirits were high, and he felt he would get well. He also had something to look forward to when he did get well. "He is talented and at Christmas time was given a piano by a Waynesboro family. He has been promised free lessons when he returns from the hospital," the newspaper reported.

While the operation was successful, it did not free Brownie from the problems of cystic fibrosis. It did give him more years to live, though how well he was able to live those years is questionable.

Brownie died on December 11, 1957, at Mt. Sinai Hospital in Baltimore. He was only twenty-one years old, and he spent the last six weeks of his life in the hospital.

"Since he was 13 years old he had been in and out of Johns Hopkins and Mt. Sinai Hospitals 15 times in the past eight years," the *Gettysburg Times* reported.

During the time since his 1950 operation, some advances had been made in the diagnosis and treatment of cystic fibrosis. In particular, the sweat test was developed and is still used today, but it didn't do Brownie any good since it is a tool for diagnosis.

He was buried in the Green Hill Cemetery in Franklin County.

Frankenstorm, Nineteenth Century Style

Hurricane Sandy in 2012 was called a "Frankenstorm" because of the devastation it wreaked, but more than a century earlier, another Frankenstorm hit the region. The Blizzard of 1888 is one of the most-famous blizzards in U.S. history.

"Although there have been many heavier snowfalls as well as significantly lower temperatures, the blizzard's combination of inclement conditions has been unmatched in more than a century," Borgna Brunner wrote in "The Great White Hurricane."

In the early days of March 1888, the weather had been typical late-winter weather with temperatures in the mid-50s.

On Sunday, March 11, temperatures began falling quickly as Arctic air from Canada met warm air from the Gulf of Mexico. The mercury stopped around six degrees above zero. The rain from the storm turned to snow and fell and fell and fell. Hurricane-strength winds gusted up to eighty miles per hour, according to the book, *A Reflection of the History of Waynesboro, Pennsylvania and Vicinity.*

"It rained at intervals all day Sunday, and towards night rain fell in torrents. The wind rose gradually until it had the velocity of a gale, and, at the same time, the temperature began to fall. At about midnight the rain turned to sleet, then to hail, finally to snow. All night long the storm raged, and when the people woke on Monday morning they saw a sight never witnessed before by even the oldest inhabitant. The city was buried under snow, and the storm still raged. The wind blew at the rate of forty miles per hour until three o'clock on Monday afternoon," reported the *Gettysburg Star and Sentinel*.

The snowfall accumulation in most areas hit by the storm was between forty and fifty inches. The fast winds made for even higher snowdrifts in some cases as tall as fifty feet. Gravesend, New York, recorded the highest drifts at fifty-two feet. Along the coast, more than 200 ships were grounded or wrecked killing at least 100 seamen, according to the National Climatic Data Center.

How the blizzard of 1888 looked in New York City. Courtesy of the Library of Congress.

Besides burying roads, the heavy snows brought down telegraph lines isolating cities throughout the Mid-Atlantic Region. The *Gettysburg Star and Sentinel* noted the blizzard blew down "200 large and valuable trees on the farm of Benj. Chambers, esq. near St. Thomas" in Franklin County.

Local newspapers also published the account of how the blizzard affected Baltimore where food supplies ran short because "not a drop of milk nor pound of produce or provisions had been received since Saturday," according to the *Gettysburg Star and Sentinel*. This was typical of what residents of Franklin County went through as well, though county farmers had easier access to food than residents in large urban areas like Baltimore.

Once the storm passed, people dug themselves out and began assessing the damage.

"Three days later, 400 people were dead, damages were estimated at $20 million and snowdrifts reached to the tops of houses from New York to New England," according to *A Reflection of the History of Waynesboro, Pennsylvania and Vicinity*. Reports don't seem to show any weather-related deaths in Franklin County from the storm.

The area was also hit with significant blizzards in 1899 and 1932, though they did not measure up to the Blizzard of 1888.

The Summer Blue Ridge Summit Burned

Blue Ridge Summit was not a heavily populated area in 1925. Only a few hundred people lived there year round, but that summer the small community suffered three fires that caused a lot of damage to the town.

On June 16, the engine house of the Monterey Hotel caught fire and burned to the ground. The loss was put at $1,000 (roughly $15,000 in 2023 dollars).

Three days later, the Chambersburg, Greencastle and Waynesboro Trolley station caught on fire. Luckily, there weren't any people there. Trolleys had been slowly falling into disuse as the popularity of cars grew. The Chambersburg, Greencastle and Waynesboro Trolley would end its service in 1928.

"The fire at Highfield Tuesday completely destroyed the confectionary story, pool room and barber shop owned by John Flautt, adjoining the station," the *Hagerstown Morning Herald* reported.

The fire department responded as quickly as it could, and Rev. Charles Niles, rector of the Episcopal Church, drove the fire truck. The problem was notifying enough people that help was needed to fight the fire. *The Gettysburg Times* called the alert system inadequate. "The old fire rings, huge iron circles with iron hammers, which were placed at various points on the mountain years ago, are now overgrown with weeds and brush and are practically useless for putting in fire calls," the newspaper reported.

The blaze was out of control by the time the firemen arrived and they concentrated on keeping the fire from spreading to nearby homes and businesses.

The trolley station suffered $1,000 in damage, while Flautt's properties had $2,500 in damage. It also caused some of the few businesses in the town to be closed for a time.

Both of these fires were reported as being suspicious.

Then in the afternoon of July 13, the shout of fire went up in one of the oldest boarding houses on the mountain, according to *The Gettysburg Times*. The boarders quickly left except for Bertha Barr, who was ill and couldn't leave her bed.

The fire department responded as quickly as it could to the scene.

"Fighting their way through stifling smoke and flames to the third story, J. M. Detrow and Dr. H. C. Bridges, of Blue Ridge Summit, yesterday afternoon rescued Miss Bertha Barr, of Baltimore, from fire which destroyed the boarding house owned by Mrs. Mae Truitt, for a time threatened the heart of the fashionable Blue Ridge Summit summer colony, and fought by a bucket brigade including girls summering at the resort," *The Gettysburg Times* reported.

The entire building burned to the ground in half an hour. Sparks from the fire set a nearby vacation lodge on fire and threatened to catch other buildings on fire, but the Waynesboro Fire Department arrived on scene and helped the Blue Ridge Summit firefighters get the fire under control.

The boarding house had recently undergone some repairs and was valued at $18,000 (roughly $300,000 in 2023 dollars). The loss was only partially covered by insurance, and Truitt had a loss of $12,000. The fire was believed to have been caused by a defective flue in the chimney by the roof.

If there was a silver lining to all the fires that summer, it is that enough money was raised to purchase a new siren for the Blue Ridge Summit Fire Department.

"It was bought after several destructive fires had threatened the entire mountain settlement because of an inadequate alarm system," *The Gettysburg Times* reported.

The new electric alarm weighed 550 pounds and was installed on a steel tower in the plaza at Blue Ridge Summit in mid-August.

First Tornado in a Century Hits Chambersburg

Monday, May 12, 1980, was winding down. Families were sitting down to dinner. Some people were just returning home from work. It has been a warm day, so many people had opened their windows to allow the fresh air in.

Then, just after 6 p.m., a large black cloud moved in over Chambersburg, Pennsylvania. The wind began gusting at incredible speeds and rain fell, sometimes heavily.

"It was like fire rolling over the top of the building. The power lines started snapping like candy," said a motorist who pulled into The Lumber Yard when the rain became too intense to see through, according to the *Chambersburg Public Opinion*.

Another Chambersburg resident, Ida Beard, said, "I was driving home (via) Radio Hill around 6 and saw a round ball in the sky to my left. It kept getting smaller. I looked like a tunnel to the sky."

Joann Davis said a "loud" and "funny" noise alerted her to something different with the storm. When she looked outside, she "saw a round ball in the sky." She also saw two motorcyclists exit Interstate 81, drive into a cornfield, and throw themselves onto the ground.

Within moments, a tornado touched down in Chambersburg and Fayetteville and "ripped its way through the area last evening, tearing apart buildings and mangling power lines," reported the *Public Opinion*. The tornado destroyed or damaged homes along Mill Road and businesses along Wayne Avenue. Four families were left homeless and three people reported minor injuries, mostly from flying glass.

The *Waynesboro Record Herald* reported that one family returned from a trip to their home on Mill Road. With the rain coming down in sheets and the wind gusting, they decided to stay in their car until the rain let up. "As they watched, most of their home was ripped away by the twister," the *Record Herald* reported.

In Fayetteville, wind and falling trees damaged two houses and a church. It damaged thirteen homes and eleven businesses in Chambersburg.

It was the first tornado in the area in more than a century. Chambersburg Mayor William Stover declared a state of emergency for the city. National Guardsmen, state and local police and firefighters stood guard in blacked-out areas of the city to prevent looking. A dawn-to-dusk curfew was declared in the Wayne Avenue area.

Borough Manager Julio Lecuona suggested that the power lines that were downed winds blew the roofs off the buildings and wrapped themselves around the power lines, turning the debris into sails. This caused the power outage, but the downed power lines also trapped some people in buildings who didn't want to venture out and risk the wind bringing a live power line in contact with them.

All the homes and businesses without power were restored within two day, but rebuilding the damaged buildings took much longer. Shops in K-Mart Plaza, American Can, Chambersburg Livestock, The Lumber Yard, and various restaurants all suffered damage.

Damage estimates quickly rose to around $3 million, though the state and federal governments did not declare the area a disaster area.

THE COUNTY AT WAR

Chambersburg Takes Sides in the Civil War

Though Chambersburg, Pennsylvania, is better known for being burned by Confederate troops in 1864, it was a hub of activity from the beginning of the war.

Fort Sumter in South Carolina surrendered to Confederate forces on April 14, 1861, marking the start of the Civil War. A few days later, on April 18, residents of Chambersburg held a ceremony to erect a 120-foot-tall flag pole on the Diamond, and a large flag fluttered from it.

"The occasion was made memorable by the singing of 'The Star Spangled Banner' by a band of patriotic ladies in front of the Franklin Hotel, and the delivery of soulthrilling speeches by Messrs. McClure, Stumbaugh, Reilly, Brewer, Everett, Stenger and Welsh. This pole stood as a witness of the patriotic impulses of the people of the community until Gen. Imboden's rebel cavalry cut it down as they were following the rear of Lee's army to Gettysburg," according to the *History of Franklin County* published in 1887.

The next day, 150 Franklin County men formed the Chambers Artillery unit and became the first Civil War unit formed in Franklin County. The men boarded a rail car on the Cumberland Valley Railroad and headed to Camp Curtin in Harrisburg.

One soldier wrote a letter to *the Pennsylvania Daily Telegraph* in Chambersburg on April 30, 1861. He noted that, "This usually quiet town now presents a very animated and soldier like appearance, as the sound of the drum, the running to and fro of soldiers, and all the pomp and circumstance of glorius (sic) war, are the distinguishing features of our streets."

Chambersburg during the Civil War. Courtesy of the Franklin County Historical Society – Kittochtinny.

As the country got onto its war footing, Marylanders headed north.

"It has been but three weeks since the stars and stripes, as everywhere in the North, came up like a rash all over the town. Two weeks ago these stars and stripes were almost the first to gladden the eyes of loyal fugitives, seeking safety in the North," the *New York World* reported on May 14, 1861, from Chambersburg.

Despite the Union loss at Fort Sumter, optimism and

support remained high in the Union. The same was also true in Chambersburg. The Union soldier writing to the newspaper reported, "The citizens of Chambersburg have been generous in their contributions, and profuse in their kindness to the soldiers and officers; while the ladies, God bless them, smile upon us so sweetly as almost to captivate us all. Their kindness will be a theme of praise among the soldiers now in Camp Curtin in future years. Although not in secret, I fear some of the fair damsels have 'laid siege' to the hearts of the gallant beaux in our comp., and may furnish a romance or a reality for the future novelist. They no doubt pity the noble fellows; but they should remember the poet says 'pity is akin to love.'"

This near innocence and unwavering optimism would soon be challenged as the war hit close to home.

Fleeing Marylanders sought refuge in Chambersburg

When the Civil War split the nation in April of 1861, Chambersburg found itself firmly on the side of the Union. Within days of the outbreak of war, a company of soldiers had formed and gone to Harrisburg to train.

However, Chambersburg had its own military camps. Camp Irvin was at the fairgrounds. "Camp Irvin, Camp McAllen and Camp Givens all occupied the same spot within a space of five weeks. The first men moved in on April 25, 1861 and Camp Givens broke up about May 30, 1861. As one group moved out and another moved in on the same day the camp changed its name that day," Lee Hoover wrote in a paper for the Kittochtinny Historical Society called "Civil War Camps In and About Chambersburg."

One soldier wrote a letter to the *Pennsylvania Daily Telegraph* in Chambersburg on April 30, 1861. He noted that, "Spectators all express surprise at the rapid improvement in the drill of the men. You see no straggling soldiers about town, but every one is compelled to attend closely to duty–a state of things which I have failed to see in other camps I have visited in the State.... While some may complain of the severe discipline, yet all must admit that constant drill alone secures efficiency, and we therefore hear constant praise awarded the General Commanding for his firmness and ambition in making the regiments under his command a credit to the service."

By the end of April, a more-permanent location for a military camp was found east of Chambersburg on the Eberly Farm (next to the current Chambersburg Hospital). The site was called Camp Slifer in honor of the Pennsylvania State Secretary Eli Slifer.

Camp Slifer was located east of Chambersburg. Courtesy of Wikimedia Commons.

The *New York World* described the camp as "long, low tenements of boards, divided by a partition into two rows of compartments, serve as barracks. At the lower end of each of these rows, until lately, an unhoused cooking stove, the center of attraction at meal times, aided in all weathers the humble picnic of the soldier. But on a second visit, you might see how the stove, with its lofty pipe, had served the carpenter a good turn. Every stove has become the nucleus of a fine shanty and was now invisible. The carpenter knew by the stove just where to put the house, and the high pipe showed him the very spot for the chimney. At the foot of the slope runs a brook, winding across the whole breadth for the encampment."

The 7th, 8th, and 10th Pennsylvania Volunteers were stationed in the camp.

Though Maryland was in the Union, many Northerners didn't feel safe below the Mason-Dixon Line. The *World* reported that "looking southward, nothing was to be seen but the trackless, raging sea of secession, from which a number were escaping..." People boarded trains and headed north, many of them reaching Chambersburg.

On May 10, 1861, "thousands" of residents gathered to watch many of the soldiers who had been quartered around the town leave to serve their country. A few hours later, those same residents got a surprise.

"Then, at one o'clock, there was a hurried drive of omnibuses through the main street, filled with the regulars from Harper's Ferry; and as the news spread of their arrival, and of the destruction of the arsenal, there was a new sensation. The men of Jones's command alighted, muddy, bedraggled and footsore. But, first of all, their hunger was to be satisfied. The neighbors had dined, but men, women and children came running to the depot with such as they had," the *World* reported.

Federal troops had withdrawn from Harpers Ferry nearly a month earlier after 1st Lt. Roger Jones set fire to the federal arsenal in the town in an effort to keep the military materiel out of the hands of the Confederate troops.

Now, the once confident people of Chambersburg became panicked. Jones' men moved on to Carlisle and the soldiers remaining were ill equipped to defend the town. So the residents waited nervously for an invasion that didn't come.

Chambersburg would eventually be occupied by Confederate forces three times during the war.

Medal of Honor Purchased for a Dime

Hugh Krebs of Chambersburg was a collector, so it seemed only natural that he would become an antiques dealer. He could prowl yard sales, flea markets, and estate auctions looking for trinkets and treasures that caught his eye.

In 1946, Krebs was "nosing through items," that were offered for sale at an auction in Adams County. A box of loose and small items had been set aside because nobody had been interested in them. It was a "junk" box, according to the *Chambersburg Public Opinion*. However, it was also selling for only a dime.

Since he was a general collector and not searching for anything in particular, Krebs rooted through the box to see if it was even worth a dime. Inside, he found a piece of history. It was a 19th century Congressional Medal of Honor.

Krebs soon found out that even among Congressional Medals of Honor, the one he had found stood alone. "A Congressional Medal of Honor, the only one awarded to a soldier who disobeyed orders in a time of war, ends up in a box of worthless trinkets and junk to be sold for ten cents," Pete Ritter wrote in the *Public Opinion*.

The Medal of Honor that Krebs purchased for 10 cents had been bought through the preservation of soldiers' lives and a Union artillery line during the Battle of Gettysburg.

On the third day of the battle, Capt. William E. Miller

from Carlisle, Pennsylvania, commanded four companies of the Third Pennsylvania Cavalry. He was sick and barely able to sit in his saddle, but he hoped that he and his men wouldn't be engaged in any fighting that day. Miller's commander had ordered him to hold his position in the woods along Low Dutch Road, southeast of Gettysburg, under any conditions.

William Miller.

From his position, Miller watched as Confederate cavalry began assembling into eight regiments. He could also see what was drawing them together. The Confederate cavalrymen were going to try to break through the Union line to destroy the artillery pieces that were pounding their fellow soldiers engaged in Pickett's Charge.

It was possible that they would succeed. The Confederate cavalry outnumbered the Michigan cavalry, which were the only defenders between them and the Union artillery.

"The Michigan cavalry mustered to charge the onrushing sabres of the Confederate horsemen when Capt. Miller, seeing the obvious strategy, turned to his first lieutenant, William Rhawl Brook, asking his support in disobeying the order to hold fast at that point. Brook agreed," Ritter wrote.

Miller led the charge of the Third Pennsylvania. The Confederate cavalry was focused on the Michigan cavalry and didn't see the charge on their flank until it was too late. The Third Pennsylvania split the Confederate line, disrupting the Confederate charge. Rather than a penetrating charge through the Union line, the Confederate cavalrymen quickly found themselves engaged in close quarters sabre battles.

Miller was wounded in the battle with what he laughed off as "a little hole in the arm." Though his role in the action was not mentioned in the official records, it was not forgotten. "In July 1897, the Congressional Medal of Honor was bestowed upon Capt. Miller by President McKinley and presented by Secretary of War Russell A. Alger, who as a colonel in the Fifth Michigan Cavalry witnessed the battle," Ritter wrote.

Miller died in 1919 and is buried in National Cemetery in Gettysburg.

How the medal came to be in a junk box sold at auction is not known. Krebs sought out any descendants of Miller's but didn't find anyone.

Once it became known that Krebs had the medal, different historical societies and the Carlisle American Legion made offers to buy it from him. He turned them all down. Once Krebs learned the story behind the medal, he knew that it was worth more than 10 cents. It was priceless.

Love and Honor in a Time of War

When Samuel Cormany left Franklin County in 1859, his country was united. He returned to find it split in two and a decision to make that hundreds of thousands of other men had made and were making. With his family barely started, should he risk his life in a war between the states?

Cormany returned to Franklin County in August 1862. Since he had been gone, he had gone to college, married, had a child and lived in Canada. His time away had changed his viewpoint of the world and his physical appearance. The first family he stopped in to see on his way home was his half-sister Lydia and her husband Henry Rebok who lived near Mechanicsburg.

"Sister Lydia didn't recognize me, nor did Henry—not knowing anything of our coming—and my being away since early in 1859—and I having growing quite a beard, and here was a woman and a baby. But soon the greetings were profuse—and time was well put in asking and answering questions," Cormany wrote in his diary.

A few days later, he was back in Franklin County and reuniting with other family members who lived nearby. One place he visited was the farm where he had grown up. His father no longer ran it, having died years before, but it was still in the family. Cormany's brother, John, farmed the land and lived in the house. Visiting the farm hit Cormany with a wave of nostalgia.

"All things look Old Home like—The old well & Pump

seem precious—O Thou precious cooling refreshing invigorating fountain, how often thou hast given me nerve when week from toil and thirst—Yes Tippy—the Dog knows me—and seems so glad & frisky—I did up The Barn—Tannery—Orchard—Meadow and Farm. My! how memories of boyhood days and pranks, their toils, and amusements come scampering along," Cormany wrote.

Samuel Cormany.

Another place Cormany, his wife Rachel, and baby Cora visited was the home of Cormany's half-brother's father-in-law. The Strocks were long-time family friends. Not only had Bernard Cormany married one of the Strock girls, but Cormany had courted one of them, too. Her name was Lydia and she and Samuel had broken up when he left for college.

"It was a little embarrassing for here was Lydia—whom I had courted so long in this home and gave up only because she had declared she never would go west nor far away from her parents for any man—so I responded 'Well then my dear we had as well close up our courtship' and it was closed in a few months, very tenderly—and here I was visiting in the Family in the same rooms we so often sat together in 3 years ago and here was also My darling Wife and Our precious little daughter—while I could not avoid thinking of the past, and the great pleasure I often had enjoyed there in her company—Yet there came up not even a twinge of regret for I am O so satisfied and happy in my Precious wife and our child," Samuel wrote.

Samuel truly was happy to be back in Franklin County, but the year was 1862 and the United States was caught up in the Civil War. Politics and war was mentioned more often in his diary entries, showing that it was more often on his mind when he thought about the events of the day he would write down.

The more he thought about, the more he came to realize that he needed to make a decision. He needed to choose a side in the war. His choice would affect not only him, but it might leave his wife a widow and his daughter fatherless. He had only been home three weeks before he decided to join the Union Army.

In September 1862, Samuel Cormany joined the Union Army. "The fear of being drafted, if I did not volunteer—had possible some weight in inducing decision," Cormany wrote in his diary.

However, a larger part of the decision was that the war was on everyone's minds and stirring a need for a person to do his or her patriotic duty. The war was talked about in churches and around dinner tables. Occasionally, army units would pass through Chambersburg on their way to a new duty station like the battery unit rumbled through the town on

Sept. 7, heading for Baltimore.

While this interaction with the military did not cause fear among residents, one interaction did. Rumors that the Confederate army was heading in the direction of Chambersburg were spreading. On Sept. 7, Cormany wrote that the rumor in town was that the rebels were near Hagerstown.

Rachel Cormany and her daughter, Cora.

Two days later, after lots of discussions and prayers with his wife, Rachel, Cormany headed into Chambersburg to enlist. "The air is full of calls for men who are patriotic to enlist—I really inwardly feel that I want to go and do my part—as a Man—as a Volunteer—leaving others to wait and be drafted—and Darling is likeminded," Cormany wrote.

He enlisted in Captain William Sullenberger's cavalry company. Sullenberger was a master carpenter in town who had served a three-month enlistment in the army in the fall of 1861 as part of Battery A, First Pennsylvania Artillery, as a lieutenant. Early in the summer of 1862, he had accepted a captain's commission on the condition that he recruit enough men to make up his company, the Sixteenth Pennsylvania Cavalry (Volunteers).

Cormany's first duty immediately after enlisting was to help recruit other men into the company to reach a full complement of men. However, even with this easy duty, he and his comrades slept with their rifles because the town was placed under martial law on Sept. 11. Families started fleeing the area because of word that the Confederate Army was moving north from Hagerstown.

"People are awfully scared—Many are leaving town—poor fools—When I came uptown to Henrys (Reboks) [Cormany's brother-in-law] they had partly packed up to leave—I set to making fun of them. Then they unpacked again concluding to remain quietly in town and see!" Cormany wrote in his diary.

Despite being convinced to stay on Sept. 12, the Reboks still left the next day because of the worry of being caught in the middle of a battle.

The Battle of Antietam occurred on Sept. 17 and the sounds of the cannons firing on the armies nearly 40 miles to the south. This only heightened the tension in Chambersburg.

After a delay of getting started, the Sixteenth Pennsylvania Cavalry (Volunteers) finally left for Harrisburg on Sept. 19 and Cormany would not return home for nearly three years.

In August 1865, Cormany wrote of his homecoming to Chambersburg and his family. "O what a joy to press my Darlings to my bosom and know that now we can plan to be together. Yes! Day by day to be at home, together, and live with and for each other," Cormany wrote in his diary.

Rachel Cormany wrote in her own diary of her husband's return, "Joy to the world—My little world at least. I am no more a war widow—My Precious is home safe from the war. I am so thankful that he is once more home & that to stay. I am happy all the time now. I do not feel now as if I were alone in the world—as I had so often to feel during his three years absence & now that the war is over I hope we can once get to our home & live as God intends we should."

Farm Wife Kept Secret From Confederate Occupiers

Mrs. Samuel Lightner would never have considered herself an actress. She was a wife and a mother of eight, and filling those roles was enough for anyone. However, in late June 1863, she performed a role worthy of the best actresses of the time.

Although her family supported the Union and her husband was in the army, Mrs. Lightner played the role of a Confederate sympathizer in order to save a railroad. Samuel Lightner had been drafted in 1862 as Chambersburg, Pennsylvania, worried about a Confederate invasion from Washington County.

For nearly a year, Mrs. Lightner had worked hard to keep the family farm near Greenville running and to care for her eight children.

At the end of June 1863, a group of Confederate scouts rode up to the farmhouse asking to be fed. Mrs. Lightner had only a few minutes to decide. She "was fearful of displeasing the southern soldiers lest they retaliate by setting fire to the home," according to the *Public Opinion*. Part of the fear certainly came from worrying about the safety of her children, but Mrs. Lightner also knew she was hiding a secret that she needed to protect.

Her decision made, she welcomed the soldiers and allowed them to camp on her farm. According to Benjamin Lightner, who was a youngster at the time, his mother spent the next week baking twenty-five loaves of bread for the soldiers and supplying each man with a pint of milk.

At the end of the month, the soldiers headed east where they would participate in the Battle of Gettysburg.

When word of what Mrs. Lightner had done leaked out, she experienced a lot of criticism among her neighbors. It wasn't until years later that it became known that Emmanuel Hale, Mrs. Lightner's father and an employee of the Cumberland Valley Railroad, had brought bonds owned by railroad to the farmhouse and asked his daughter to hide them. She had done so, and this was another reason she had needed to keep the Confederate soldiers from searching the house or burning it down.

The Cumberland Valley Railroad was an early railroad that was chartered in 1831 and connected to Pennsylvania's Main Line. It ran from Harrisburg to Chambersburg down to Hagerstown, Maryland, and Winchester, Virginia. In 1839, it became the first railroad to have passenger sleeping cars. The railroad had been used to supply Union troops during the war.

The Confederate Army had already shown a willingness to destroy the railroad when soldiers tore down railway buildings in Chambersburg in 1862 around the same time Samuel Lightner was drafted. At the time Mrs. Lightner was hiding the securities, the Confederate Army was burning the railroad's property in Chambersburg and torn up miles of track. A year after this incident, the Confederate Army under Jubal Early returned to Chambersburg and burned even more of the railroad's property.

One of the Lightner children, Mrs. W.F. Kohler of Scotland, Pennsylvania, told the story of the reason her mother had helped the Confederates to the *Public Opinion* in the early 1950s.

Chambersburg's Role in the War of 1812

The War of 1812 came as no surprise to the residents of Franklin County, Pennsylvania. In the early 1800s, the British had been increasingly aggressive towards the United States. The British Navy essentially kidnapped Americans and forced them into the Royal Navy. The British government supported American Indian tribes that fought against American expansion, particularly in Canada.

With each new aggressive action, Franklin County residents held their collective breath, waiting for a declaration of war. When it came, it was followed by a call to arms to among the men in Franklin County.

Among the companies raised, according to I. H. M'Cauley in *Historical Sketch of Franklin County, Pennsylvania*, were the Antrim Greens rifle company, the Franklin County Light Dragoons, the Mercersburg Rifles, the Concord Light Infantry and the Chambersburg Union Volunteers.

Congress declared war on the British on June 18, 1812, the first time the U.S. government had taken this action. The first Franklin County troops left on Sept. 5 to help defend the country. The group was made up of 264 soldiers and officers from the companies that had formed prior to the war.

While exemplary, Samuel Penniman Bates and Jacob Fraise Richard wrote the *History of Franklin County, Pennsylvania*, "The quota of the county was 507, and the deficiency was made up by draft from the militia. Maj. William

McClellan was in command of the detachment."

The men were sent to the northwest, reaching Meadville in late September. There, the Franklin County companies reorganized into four regiments—two rifle regiments and two infantry regiments. The regiments formed a Franklin County brigade commanded by General Adamson Tannahill. From the Meadville, the brigade was sent to Buffalo, New York.

Franklin County soldiers participated in the Battle of Chippewa during the War of 1812. Courtesy of Wikimedia Commons.

Another draft took place in 1814, with Franklin County expected to supply 215 men. Capt. Samuel Dunn of Path Valley had a company of forty men that volunteered, and the rest were drafted and sent to Loudon, New Hampshire, in March. Major McClellan took command of the soldiers and led them to Erie.

Thomas Poe of Antrim joined the regiment at Erie, Pennsylvania. Bates and Richard call him "a brave and gallant soldier. He was a man born to command. It is told of him that by the mere power of his presence he quelled an outbreak of his men in camp, and by a word forced them to go quietly to their quarters."

In 1814, Gen. Jacob Brown was ordered to cross the Niagara River and seize Fort Erie and advance north to Chippewa. The American army was 4,000 men strong, including the Franklin County regiments.

Capturing the fort was easy. Fort Erie only had 137 men.

Unfortunately, there were 2,500 British soldiers nearby.

As the Americans moved north, they encountered the British advance guard at the Chippewa River. On July 5, Brown ordered the Indians in his army and Pennsylvania volunteers to clear out the woods between the Chippewa River and Street's Creek. Rather than clearing out the small advance guard, they encountered the main British army.

During the ensuing battle, the Americans, particularly the Pennsylvania riflemen, showed their effectiveness. They laid down heavy and effective fire that broke the British attack. The British lost 148 men. Another 321 were wounded.

The Americans had 350 wounded and 60 men killed, including Poe. He was wounded during the fighting on July 5 and died the next day.

When the British burned Washington D.C. in August 1814, it inspired patriotic spirit. Amid this spirit, messengers were sent to U.S. government representatives asking whether additional troops were needed.

The first messenger arrived back in Chambersburg at midnight one evening and found a crowd waiting despite the late hour. "The bells were rung, the town aroused, and the drum and fife called the people to arms," M'Cauley wrote. "In a few days seven companies were fully organized and equipped to march to Baltimore."

Franklin County men responded, including a troop of Mercersburg cavalry under Capt. Mathew Patton. However, when the men reached Baltimore, they were told that cavalry wasn't needed, "but the majority of the troops determined to go to the war, disposed of their horses, and joined different companies of infantry," wrote Bates and Richard.

By 1815, both sides occupied territory of the other, but the Treaty of Ghent restored the boundaries back to what they had been prior to the war. The treaty ended the war and the Franklin County volunteers were mustered out and returned home.

ODDS & ENDS

Odds & Ends

The Boys of the Blue Ridge

The calls of "Play Ball" soon follow spring's arrival. The region has its share of amateur teams and leagues, but there was a time when the region had professional baseball players.

South of the Mason Dixon Line in Washington County, Maryland, Charles Boyer, a former president of the South Atlantic Baseball League, had moved back to the Hagerstown, Maryland, area in 1914. He watched the town teams playing against each other and saw that there was talent among the players that deserved to be rewarded.

He purchased the Hagerstown baseball team and set to work, forming a new baseball league that would soon be named the Blue Ridge League. A competition was held throughout the area to name the new league. Arthur Schellhase, a Chambersburg railroader, is the person who won the competition with "Blue Ridge League." He won out over such entries as "Apple Blossom League" (not very manly), "Mason and Dixon League" (not too bad), "Potomac League" (a little too south), and "Marpawva League" (too much of a mouthful).

In March 1915, National Commission President John K. Tener, who also a former Pennsylvania governor, accepted the application of the Blue Ridge League to be recognized as a professional league. It was given Class D status, the lowest level of professional baseball at the time, according to the website, Class D Blue Ridge League.

"It was entry level baseball," says Robert Savitt, author

of *The Blue Ridge League* and a Myersville resident. "Even though the players got paid, they still needed to have other jobs."

As the teams set about recruiting players, they had little to offer despite the fact they were professional teams.

Charles Boyers, president of the Blue Ridge Baseball League. Courtesy of Wikimedia Commons.

Each team could have no more than thirteen players, which included the required player-manager. The total monthly salary cap was $1,300 a month. That's about $32,000 in today's dollars and some clubs didn't even have a cap that high. Frederick lost the chance of having Ty Cobb's younger brother play for the Hustlers because the team had already reached its $500 a month salary cap, according to the *Frederick Post.*

In Chambersburg, Pennsylvania, Clay "Pop" Henninger was a businessman whose store sold men's hats and furnishings, but he had also played for the Chambersburg team in the Cumberland Valley League in the 1890s. He would serve as president of the Chambersburg Maroons for seven years. Chambersburg would field a team for all but one year that the Blue Ridge League played, although for the last two seasons, the team was called the Young Yanks.

By the time that the league was ready for its inaugural season, there were six teams in the league from Chambersburg, Gettysburg, and Hanover in Pennsylvania; Hagerstown and Frederick in Frederick, and Martinsburg in West Virginia. The team to win the most games during the season would be the pennant winner.

By mid-August 1915, the Hustlers had clinched the first pennant for the Blue Ridge League with six scheduled games left.

"They have obtained such a lead in the last month that it will not be necessary to play off the several postponed and tie games," the *Frederick Daily News* Reported.

The Hustlers finished the season with a record of 53-23-1. The team also finished the season with the top hitter and pitcher in the league. Bobbie Orrison from Brunswick, Maryland, was an outfielder with a .341 batting average. Bill King of Jefferson was the pitcher with seventeen wins.

1915 Chambersburg Maroons. Courtesy of Robert Savitt.

Over the years, there would be other name changes for teams.
- Chambersburg had the Maroons and Young Yanks.
- Frederick had the Hustlers, Champs and Warriors.
- Hagerstown had the Blues, Terriers, Champs and Hubs.
- Hanover had the Hornets and Raiders.
- Martinsburg had the Champs, Blue Sox and Mountaineers.
- Waynesboro had the Red Birds and Villagers.

Teams also dropped out of the league because of financial pressures, and other teams would take their place, such as Waynesboro. Sometimes a team would drop out and then come back in under new ownership for a later season.

Entering its third season, the Blue Ridge League faced two major problems in 1918. The World War I draft continued to make soldiers of many of the players, making it hard to field a team. The Blue Ridge League was the only Class D league that even attempted a season. It had only four teams that year, down from its usual six. In addition, the Spanish Flu sickened and sometimes killed both players and fans. Because of these problems, the Blue Ridge League's 1918 season ended after only three weeks.

The league did not resume play until 1920.

When the league reorganized after the war, Waynesboro, Pennsylvania, was a new entry filling the place previously held by Gettysburg. Kenneth Potter ran an insurance business and loved baseball. They played on the E-B Field on Antietam Street, although improvements hurriedly had to be made to make it suitable for the town's first professional baseball team.

Though the Major League teams recruited players from the Blue Ridge League, the teams remained independent. As the Blue Ridge League teams struggled financially, some dropped out of the league and others had to be added in order to maintain professional status.

In the late-1920's, the teams began agreeing to Major League ownership. Not only would the Major League team financially support the small Blue Ridge League teams, but they would also lend the prestige of their names to the smaller teams.

"The Blue Ridge League was the pioneer in the formation of the farm system," Savitt said.

In 1929, the Cleveland Indians purchased the Hustlers, and the team changed its name to the Warriors, which was a better match with the parent team. The Indians had already plucked a Hustler from Frederick (Ray Gardner) years earlier and were hoping to develop more players in the future. The Indians even came to Frederick to play an exhibition game with the Warriors in June 1929.

"Having the Major League teams play exhibition games really generated fan interest," said Savitt.

The New York Yankees purchased the Maroons, which is why Babe Ruth came to Chambersburg with the Yankees for an exhibition game. Following the purchase, Maroons became the Young Yanks.

Though the Blue Ridge League was on the lowest rung of professional baseball, it had a lasting impact on baseball besides introducing the farm system to the sport. The league also pioneered playing night games under bright lights and playing games on Sunday. The latter actually led to players being arrested for violating Blue Laws.

Savitt says that he can count at least 100 Major League players who played for some time in the Blue Ridge League, Three future Hall of Famers took their first steps in the league: pitcher Lefty Grove (Martinsburg, 1920), outfielder Hack Wilson (Martinsburg, 1921-'22) and umpire Bill McGowan (1917). Besides this, Bill Allington (Chambersburg, 1926), the most successful manager in All-American Girls Professional Baseball League history, gained induction into the Hall with the rest of the league.

- 1915 Frederick Hustlers
- 1916 Chambersburg Maroons
- 1917 Hagerstown Terriers
- 1918 Cumberland Colts
- 1919 *Season suspended*
- 1920 Hagerstown Champs
- 1921 Frederick Hustlers
- 1922 Martinsburg Blue Sox
- 1923 Martinsburg Blue Sox
- 1924 Martinsburg Blue Sox
- 1925 Hagerstown Hubs
- 1926 Hagerstown Hubs
- 1927 Chambersburg Maroons
- 1928 Hanover Raiders

- 1929 Hagerstown Hubs
- 1930 Chambersburg Young Yanks

Despite the support of Major League ownership, the Blue Ridge Teams continued to struggle.

"With the stock market crash in 1929, a lot of Major League team owners lost money and could no longer support the Blue Ridge teams and the league never came back from that," Ziegler says.

The longest-running Class D baseball league ended its run on February 10, 1930.

A few attempts were made to revive the league in the 1930s and 1940s, but these leagues lasted only a few seasons and were never more than semi-pro.

Brother vs. Brother Leads to Death

When Cain slew his brother Abel, it was over who was more beloved by God. When Samuel Shockey killed his brother Jacob, it was over who a young woman named Iva Wills loved more.

Iva was Jacob's common-law wife or girlfriend, depending on who you asked. She was an attractive, petite redhead who had met Jacob in Ohio and returned with him when he returned to his hometown of Beartown, Pennsylvania, in March 1924.

The son of a Monterey merchant, Jacob, who was 30 years old, had enlisted in the Army under a fake name and served in the Fourteenth U.S. Infantry at Columbus, Ohio, according to the *Gettysburg Times*. He had deserted and then re-enlisted in the Eleventh U.S. Cavalry about a year later under his own name in Columbus. It was during his time in Ohio that he met Iva, who would have been in her early teens.

After his enlistment was up, Jacob worked for a year as a Michigan State Trooper. He returned to Beartown in 1924 with Iva, who was now 19 years old. He worked odd jobs and drank too much. While drunk, he would sometimes hit Iva or threaten to shoot her.

They weren't back in Beartown for too long before Iva had had enough. On March 20, 1924, after Jacob struck her and then went out hunting, Iva left their house and found

Samuel Shockey. Iva told Samuel her story, and he took her someplace safe. The two of them were walking down the mountain when they met up with thirteen-year-old Katherine Woodring.

The three of them continued walking toward Katherine's home when they met up with Jacob. He had returned home and found Iva gone. He set off in search of her, threatening several people as he questioned them and ranted about finding Iva.

According to court testimony, both brothers were armed, but Jacob had his rifle raised, and Samuel was forced to lay down his shotgun. Jacob hit Iva, and when Samuel intervened, Jacob hit him with the butt of his rifle.

That started a fist fight between the brothers as they fought for control of the rifle, which had gotten flung away from them. Katherine ran away in a panic, but Iva tried to separate the two men who were rolling around on the ground exchanging blows.

Jacob managed to retrieve his rifle and fired two shots at his brother, missing him. Samuel scurried away and managed to get his shotgun and aim it at his brother. According to Samuel's court testimony, Jacob taunted him, saying that he was afraid to shoot. Samuel said that Jacob was actually preparing to fire when Samuel was forced to shoot him.

The shot killed Jacob.

Samuel panicked. He was already wanted for forgery in Waynesboro. He grabbed Iva's hand, and they fled toward the home of Clyde Quilley further up the mountain when they heard people coming drawn by the sound of the shots.

The pair ran back down the trail where they dragged Jacob's body off to the side and covered it with brush. Then they ran off in another direction to find a place to hide.

The group hadn't been drawn by the shots but by Katherine's warning of the armed brothers fighting. As the group came down the trail, Elmer Shockey, one of Jacob's and Samuel's brothers, found Jacob's body.

The Pennsylvania State Police formed a posse. During the manhunt, Sheriff Merle Ankerbrand's car broke down, causing his group to turn back to Waynesboro. Tracking dogs were brought in, but with five inches or more of snow on the ground, they weren't able to help.

Elmer led the posse to a small shelter where Samuel had operated a still. If Samuel had hidden there, he was gone by the time the posse arrived. They met a boy who told them he had seen Samuel and a girl the previous night, and he gave them directions to where he had seen them.

"Before them was a tent. A thin, smoking stove pipe protruded from the roof. A man emerged from the tent, gathered a handful of wood and re-entered. That man was Samuel Shockey," the *Gettysburg Times* reported.

Corporal McCarthy silently approached the tent as the other men surrounded the clearing and slowly moved in. McCarthy threw back the tent flap and shoved his rifle into Samuel's face. Before McCarthy could say anything Constable Klipp lunged through the opening in the tent, tackled Samuel and pinned him to the ground.

"I never thought anybody would be fool enough to come after me on a day like this," the newspaper reported.

A murderer is murdered

Samuel Shockey shot and killed his brother, Jacob, in March 1924. There was no doubt about that. Samuel admitted it when he was arrested.

What was in question was whether or not it was self-defense.

That's what Samuel claimed when the police arrested him

on March 21. He sat in the Franklin County Jail while awaiting trial. Meanwhile, hundreds of people turned out for the viewing of Jacob's body. These weren't all family and friends of Jacob. Many of them were people who were just curious about the case of fratricide.

Jacob's wife or girlfriend, Iva Wills, had sought out Samuel after Jacob had hit her on March 20. Jacob had found them walking down a lonely mountain trail. It had led to a fist fight and then the fatal shooting of Jacob.

The case came to trial on April 30, 1924.

No one, not even Samuel, denied that he had killed his brother. Samuel had even taken the stand and testified to it. The defense tried to paint Jacob as dangerous and treacherous as witnesses testified to Jacob's violence against Iva and others.

However, Samuel's past came under scrutiny of the prosecution. In 1920, Samuel had been indicted with three others for larceny, but had been found not guilty. The following year, he and two of his brothers had been indicted for larceny. This time, he was found guilty and sentenced to six months in prison. He had escaped, but then gave himself up after being on the run for seven months. He then had to serve an additional six months for the escape. These were not violent crimes, but they showed Samuel's disregard for the law.

The jury found Samuel guilty of second-degree murder. The defense team made a motion for a new trial, but it was overturned. Edmund C. Wingerd and John W. Hoke for the defense asked for leniency in view of facts of the case and extenuating circumstances. They urged Judge Biddle to make the sentence more in line with a manslaughter conviction. District Attorney Clippinger pressed for the maximum ten- to twenty-year sentence.

Judge Biddle sentenced Jacob to nine years in Eastern

Penitentiary.

"Mr. Hoke said that there is no doubt in his mind but that if Shockey had been a man of good reputation he would have been acquitted in a few minutes by the jury under the evidence of the case," the *Gettysburg Times* reported.

Sheriff Merle Ankerbrand escorted Samuel to prison while the courts decided what to do with Iva, who had not only been a witness during the trial but had also been arrested as an accessory to Jacob's murder.

"Evidence in the case of Samuel Shockey did not incriminate the girl. In fact it was said in the course of the testimony that she tried to separate the quarreling brothers," the newspaper reported.

Most people believed that she and Samuel were in love, which could have also been a motive for the murder. She was eventually released without being charged.

After a little more than three years in prison, Samuel had become a trustee and was granted extra privileges. One evening, he escaped from the convict barracks at Graterford. He was traced to the home of Charles Wade in Cascade, Maryland, on February 3, 1928, but all the officers found was Samuel's prison uniform.

His escape caused concern because Samuel had threatened the people of Beartown who had testified for the prosecution during his trial. Some of the families moved away rather than wait to see if Samuel would come for them.

On Feb. 11, Samuel, who was hiding out near Beartown, talked to his brother, Christian Shockey, and said that he wanted to turn himself in. Samuel asked his brother to give him a shave and haircut first. They made arrangements to meet at 1:30 p.m. in the afternoon.

When Christian showed up, he found his brother lying dead on the side of the trail in a scene strangely reminiscent of when Jacob had been killed four years earlier. Samuel had been shot in the head and abdomen a probably hit on the head with an axe.

"First believed to have been a suicide, an autopsy showed that three sponge-ball bullets fired from a shotgun had put an end to the comparatively short criminal career of the mountaineer 'bad man,'" the *Gettysburg Times* reported.

Thousands of curious people turned out to view Samuel's body, perhaps to make sure the bad man of the mountains was really dead.

Forest Ranger Harry Thomas tracked down where Samuel had been hiding since his escape. It was a canvas and oilcloth shack stocked with stolen goods.

"No clues but enemies "several 'avowed enemies' of the convict, whom he had threatened for the aid which they gave state authorities after he had killed his brother four years ago," the newspaper reported.

None of those leads panned out, however, and Samuel's killer was never discovered.

The Taste of Mountain Dew

When the sale, production and transportation of alcohol was banned in the United States in 1920, Franklin Countians had to choose between becoming teetotalers or criminals. Many law-abiding citizens chose the latter.

"I remember my father telling me stories about men making moonshine up in the mountains at Caledonia. My great-grandparents had a summer home along Route 30 which included about nine acres behind the house where it was made. Grandmother would have had a fit had she known - she was a very Methodist Temperance woman," Ann Hull, executive director of the Franklin County Historical Society - Kittochtinny said.

Since a person could get in trouble buying a drink, people who did it, didn't talk about it. That didn't mean that it wasn't happening. Underground bars, or speakeasies, weren't advertised. People knew about them by word of mouth. You got in by knowing someone or knowing a password. Manufacturing moved to stills hidden in the woods.

Charlotte Ransom Butler recalled a place where illegal liquor was made and sold in her neighborhood on South Street in Chambersburg. "Although there wasn't too much notoriety or anything, I know after church at night, Sunday night, people sort of congregated there. Visitors came in from Hagerstown and all. Wes [Crunkleton] made his own liquors," Butler told C. Bernard Ruffin for his book, *An All-American Town: An Oral History of the African American*

Community of Franklin County, Pennsylvania.

Where there is a demand for something that's not being met, people find a way to meet it. The greater the unmet demand is, the more can be charged for the product. That attracted many people to become moonshiners and rumrunners. Nationwide, it gave rise to the mafia.

A moonshiner monitoring his still. Courtesy of Wikimedia Commons.

Even locally, there were gangs of bootleggers. The *Star and Sentinel* reported in 1920 that three men had been arrested as part of a larger gang of bootleggers manufacturing and selling whiskey in northern Pennsylvania. Police, operating on a tip, staked out the suspect's house in Chambersburg until he met with some other men. The police moved in, arresting three men with seventy gallons of liquor valued at $2,500 (roughly $35,000 today).

Even being in jail didn't stop some moonshiners from continuing their trade. In 1926, Walter Sprenkle of Waynesboro was caught making moonshine while he was serving a sentence for moonshining.

"Friends brought fruit, Sprenkle at the fruit after removing the peeling and then he procured himself a stone jar, in which he kept the fruit peel, adding a little water and sugar," the *Gettysburg Times* reported.

Blue Mountain House at Pen-Mar. The resorts in Pen-Mar attracted lots of moonshiners and customers. Courtesy of Wikimedia Commons.

Apparently, the smell of the concoction finally gave it away and Sheriff Ankerbrand destroyed it. He discovered that it was being made from the peels of lemons, apples, bananas and peaches.

It wasn't the first time that Sprenkle had been caught making moonshine in jail.

"Once before he was trusty and procured most of his lemons and raisins for his concoction from the jail pantry," the newspaper reported.

Pen-Mar, with its ideal location as a resort on the border between Maryland and Pennsylvania, became a popular spot for bootleggers to hide their stills. Also, being at Pen-Mar put them close to people who wanted to relax and enjoy themselves with a drink. In 1921, an informant told police that there were thirteen stills that he knew of in the vicinity of Pen-Mar. The bootleggers were making good money selling their product, though they didn't stay long in one place.

The *Gettysburg Compiler* reported that one informant to the bootlegging at Pen-Mar saw "a bootlegger with a suitcase, placed the latter on a rock near the old Blue Mountain House path and did a land office business by handing the liquor out by the pint and half pint to people who appeared from among the bushes."

After a few minutes, he closed up shop, disappeared into the woods only to reappear in another location about half an hour or so later.

Rumors circulated that citizens weren't the only ones making money from prohibition. It was said that police were getting payoffs to look the other way at drinking among upper class. When out-of-towners were caught with liquor, things could be rough, though. Liquor fines could be used to generate more income than a speed trap. In 1930, S. A. Broaddus of Lexington, Ken., caught with a quart liquor in Franklin County. He lost his car and was fined $100.

"The word has long since gone around this section of the country to keep out of Franklin county if you have any liquor about your person," the *Daily Mail* reported.

Besides illegal manufacturing of alcohol, Prohibition led to other types of crime.

For pharmacists who used alcohol in their preparations, they also had to lock them up in a secure location when the pharmacy was closed, just as they had to do with other medicines. Shoemaker's Drug Store in Chambersburg was once robbed because alcohol was kept in an alcohol vault in the basement of the building for use in medicines.

A dismantled still captured in a raid. Courtesy of the Library of Congress.

Two men broke into the pharmacy on April 8, 1929. Unfortunately for them, Wayne Shoemaker was staying in the apartment at the rear of the store. He woke up when he thought he heard voices.

"About that time the men ascended a stairway leading to the drug store and in the narrow stairway knocked a large bottle off a shelf. The bottle rolled to the base of the steps and shattered with a resounding crash. The intruders then returned to the cellar and left the building by the same cellar door they had entered," the *Public Opinion* reported.

Upon investigation of the cellar, it was found that the

would-be robbers had attempted to break into the liquor vault for something to drink. They had broken through the larger vault, but the small vault within had stopped them.

Due to its unpopularity, Prohibition soon ended after the election of Franklin D. Roosevelt in 1932.

Residents get desperate for a drink during Prohibition

In old movies, sometimes a drunk will say that he drinks liquor for "medicinal purposes only." Such an excuse dates to the Prohibition Era when although the "manufacture, sale, or transportation of intoxicating liquors" was constitutionally prohibited, alcohol could still be used by pharmacists to prepare medications.

For pharmacists who did use alcohol in their preparations, they also had to lock up alcohol in a secure location when the pharmacy was closed just as they had to do with other medicines. In the Shoemaker's Drug Store on East Queen Street and Central Avenue in Chambersburg, alcohol was kept in an alcohol vault in the basement of the building. The vault was actually a smaller vault within a larger one, both of which had locks.

On the evening of April 8, 1929, Wayne Shoemaker locked up his pharmacy and retired to the apartment at the rear of the store where he sometimes stayed. Shortly after 1 a.m. on Apr. 9, he was awakened by voices outside his window on the Central Avenue side of his store.

He suspected, at first, that it was a policeman talking to someone.

He was wrong.

Two men, Landis Reeder and Clarence "Dutch" Rohr, were the ones talking. However, the pair went to the rear of the pharmacy and went through an archway leading to Queen Street. Perhaps they were lucky or maybe they knew that the janitor of the Zullinger Building, in which Shoemaker's Drug Store was located, had retired a few days earlier and hadn't locked the basement door properly.

The padlock on the cellar door hadn't been fully attached and Reeder and Rohr could open the door and slip into the basement.

Shoemaker heard them enter the building. He quickly dressed and then moved into the front of his store, intending to call the police.

"About that time the men ascended a stairway leading to the drug store and in the narrow stairway knocked a large bottle off a shelf. The bottle rolled to the base of the steps and shattered with a resounding crash. The intruders then returned to the cellar and left the building by the same cellar door they had entered," the *Public Opinion* reported.

Shoemaker went back through the store and slipped out the door onto Central Avenue hoping to see who came out of the store cellar. He saw two men walk around the corner of the store and start towards Queen Street.

"Both were brushing dust off their clothes. Shoemaker walked ahead of them to Queen and Central avenue where there is an incandescent light," the *Public Opinion* reported. "As Reeder and Rohr passed, he said nothing but Rohr asked Reeder whether he knew the fellow standing at the pole. Reeder replied in the negative and both men turned in Queen towards Main Street."

Once they had passed, Shoemaker went to the police headquarters to report the break-in. The officers were out on patrol, though, so he called in his report and Motorcycle Officer Winger responded.

Upon investigation of the cellar, it was found that the would-be robbers had attempted to break into the liquor vault for something to drink. They had managed to break through the larger vault, but the small vault within had stopped them.

Winger began a search for the men. Reeder was found in his bed with his clothes on and Rohr was found on the porch of a friend's house. Both of them showed signs of having been drinking, but whether it is liquor they found at the pharmacy or elsewhere is unclear.

Reeder and Rohr were arrested and charged with breaking and entering with the intent to commit a felony all because they got a little thirsty.

A New Totem Pole for Totem Pole Playhouse

"**S**orry we're sold out," Lu Merriman, box office manager for Totem Pole Playhouse, told a patron days before the opening of the 1970 season in July.

While that is good news to any actor, director, or theater owner, it was particularly sweet sounding to everyone involved with Totem Pole Playhouse. The previous November, a fire had burned the playhouse to the ground. People had talked about the end of Franklin County's summer stock theater, which had first opened in 1950.

A group of eight teenagers weren't so ready to surrender to despair. They formed Teen People for Totem Pole just four days after the fire. They selected their officers and set their sights on how to achieve their goal of keeping Totem Pole Playhouse going. What that required was money to rebuild.

"Since November, they have sold candy and note paper, held a dance, and, from proceeds, have each purchased a seat in the new theater. The one-ton totem pole is the Teen People's gift to the new 400-seat theater," Jayne Thomas wrote for *The Public Opinion*.

During that time, the group donated more than $1,300 (about $7,500 today) to the theater, including $500 (about $3,000 today) right before the opening of the 1970 season.

However, as it grew more obvious that the playhouse would continue, Teen People for Totem Pole realized that something was still missing... the totem pole.

The group commissioned Donald T. Park, who specialized in "custom artistry" to carve a new pole in April 1970. Crafted from a sycamore tree donated by the Greene Township supervisors, the new totem pole stood twenty feet out of the ground and was painted in red, green, yellow, and blue billboard paints.

Jean Stapleton and William Putch after the fire at the Totem Pole Playhouse. Courtesy of the Franklin County Historical Society – Kittochtinny

The first totem at the bottom of the pole was fire to represent the destruction of the old playhouse. Above that was a bear embracing a child. The bear represented strength and resolve, and the child represented the Teen People for Totem Pole. The next totem was a beaver to represent the determination of everyone involved with the project to rebuild the playhouse. Next was a fox eating a frog, which was supposed to represent how the skeptics who said the playhouse wouldn't continue had been proven wrong. Finally, the pole was topped by the Thunderbird God whose job it was to care for the new Totem Pole Playhouse.

"Eight months ago there was fire and destruction, with bleak hopes of ever having another summer theater here. That totem pole means new beginnings," Thomas wrote.

The totem pole was installed at the playhouse on July 7, a week and a half before the grand re-opening of the theater.

The show chosen to open the new season was "Our Town," the Pulitzer-Prize-winning play by Thornton Wilder. William Putch, who is credited with helping the theater gain national recognition, directed the show. It was one of the 270 shows he produced at Totem Pole Playhouse. Actors John Beal, Tom McKenna, and Alice Elliott starred in this new performance. Putch's wife, Jean Stapleton, also had a role, though she had not yet achieved the stardom she would soon reach as Edith Bunker on the TV series "All in the Family."

"Saturday night will be the icing on the cake for so many who are attached to good summer stock theater. The new 400-seat theater at Caledonia has the distinction of being the only one of its kind build as a summer stock theater on the eastern cost," Thomas wrote.

According to the Totem Pole Playhouse website, the theater is one of only a few summer theaters that still maintains a resident company of actors. Other well-known stars who have appeared there include Keir Dullea, Sada Thompson, John Ritter, Sandy Dennis, Harry Groener, Curtis Armstrong and, of course, Stapleton.

Waynesboro Residents Get Free Home Mail Delivery

Better late than never, as they say.

The United States Post Office started experimenting with Rural Free Delivery in 1891. As the program expanded, Pennsylvania got its first two RFD routes near the end of November 1896. Nearby Shippensburg was the first RFD route near Franklin County, beginning in 1899. By 1905, the state had nearly 700 RFD routes, including ones in Carlisle, Chambersburg, Gettysburg, Mercersburg and Orrtanna.

Waynesboro, Pennsylvania, was still using the old postal system where residents had to come to the post office to get their mail. That changed on February 1, 1905, at 9 a.m. when A. Stover Fitz, Norman S. Fair and Howard M. Weaver left the Bank of Waynesboro building where the post office was located and headed out on Waynesboro's first RFD routes.

Fair and Weaver drove mail wagons while Fitz delivered the mail in a buggy.

They had been preparing for this moment for weeks. The men had taken dry runs along their routes, which would take around seven hours to complete. They had studied the regulations regarding RFD and even visited the mail sorting operation in Chambersburg, which had gotten RFD near the end of 1901.

Some of the new regulations that the mail carriers had to get used to were, according to Carl V. Besore and Robert L.

Ringer in *A Reflection of the History of Waynesboro, Pennsylvania and Vicinity*:
- The mail carriers had to keep a count of all mail picked up on the route each day.
- Any mail the carrier collected that could be delivered before returning to the post office first had to have the carrier cancel the postage with an indelible pencil.
- The carrier had to keep postage stamps, cards, stamped envelopes, and money order blanks with him. "If patrons entrusted him, the carrier could act as their agent, enclosing their money in the stamped addressed envelope given him by the patron," Besore and Ringer wrote.
- If carriers met someone who lived on their route while they were driving, they could deliver their mail to them if requested, but only if it cost them no time on their route.
- Carriers had to deliver registered mail and pension to the addressee's home as long as their mailbox was less than a mile off the route. If the house was further away, a note would be left in the mailbox explaining who could get the mail and where it could be obtained.
- Special delivery letters would be delivered to the addressee's house if it was within a mile of the mailbox. If the house was further away, the letter would be left in the mailbox as ordinary mail.

The first day of rural free delivery in Waynesboro went well. "The roads were fairly good, but Mr. Fitz decided to use a sleigh the next day. All reported many patrons greeted them at their letter boxes," Besore and Ringer wrote.

The one problem that the mail carriers ran into the first day was that they could only place mail in approved boxes, but many residents along the mail routes hadn't gotten their mailboxes yet. The postmaster gave the carriers permission to deliver mail to temporary mailboxes as long as the resident had ordered an approved mailbox.

This led to a very interesting temporary mailbox. "Carrier Fitz, upon reaching the Samuel H. Brown residence at Roadside, found an unusual mail box. An old bucket had been shined up and a U.S. flag attached to it. Brown was one who had not year received his box. He knew home-made boxes were not permissible, but he found nothing in the regulations prohibiting the use of a bucket," Besore and Ringer wrote.

A Pennsylvania mailman delivering mail in the early 1800s. Courtesy of ExplorePAHistory.com.

The mail volume among the three routes that first day were: sixty-six letters, twenty-six postcards, 128 newspapers, thirty-seven circulars, and one package delivered, and thirty-five letters, eight postcards, three money-order applications, one newspaper, and one package picked up.

Though the first day went smoothly, the second day of rural free delivery had some hiccups. The mail carriers left fifteen minutes later, probably because of heavier mail volume.

Later in the day, Fair stopped at the H. B. Motz Store in Tomstown, Pennsylvania, to write a money-order application. Some nearby sledders accidentally frightened his horse while Fair was still inside. The horse took off.

"Several men caught the animal and quieted him down, but not until he had kicked the shafts off the stick wagon. Repairs could not be made in time for Mr. Fair to finish delivery on the last one-fourth of his route, so he walked the two and one-half miles back to Waynesboro leading his horse" mail delivered the next day," Besore and Ringer wrote.

It is not noted whether anyone suggested that the Postal Service creed be changed to, "Neither snow nor rain nor heat nor gloom of night stays these couriers from the swift completion of their appointed rounds, but a frightened horse can."

More Radios Than Bathrooms in County Farms

In 1934, it seems like Franklin County, Pennsylvania, farmers were more interested in listening to radio shows like "Amos 'n Andy" than enjoying the convenience of not having to brave winter temperatures using an outhouse.

According to a Pennsylvania Department of Agriculture farm report for 1933, Franklin County farms had 720 radios and only 370 bathrooms. This is despite the fact that 730 farms had indoor running water.

The report provides a glimpse at the county's agriculture history and allows an opportunity to see how much things have changed in the last century. In that time, Franklin County has lost over two thirds of its farms, falling from 3,536 farms in 1930 to 1,300 today.

Some items produced by Franklin County farmers in 1933 included:
- 11,126,770 gallons of milk
- 2,784,680 dozens of eggs
- 2,036,370 bushels of corn
- 1,099,720 bushels of wheat
- 487,700 bushels of apples
- 279,480 bushels of potatoes
- 176,170 bushels of oats
- 165,120 bushels of rye
- 122,390 bushels of peaches
- 98,520 bushels of barley

- 83,180 pounds of wool
- 57,900 tons of hay
- 38,250 pounds of honey
- 4,630 bushels of buckwheat
- 3,560 bushels of pears

All of this was produced using 8,350 tons of fertilizer and 2,440 tons of lime.

As for livestock, county farmers raised:
- 457,210 chickens
- 24,110 swine
- 21,280 milk cows and heifers 2 years and older
- 12,700 sheep
- 10,970 other cattle
- 9,160 horses
- 2,550 beehives
- 1,490 mules

Agricultural products generated $3,510,950 for county farmers in 1932 or roughly $59 million today, and just about half of that income came from milk and dairy products. Agriculture was a growing county industry when many businesses were losing money or failing because of the Great Depression. The *Public Opinion* noted that while 1933 figures weren't available at the time, "it is anticipated that the figures will be considerably above those for 1932."

Today's farmers can take advantage of new technology like milking machines and combines. In 1932, among the 3,536 Franklin County farms were 860 trucks, 720 tractors, 1,490 gas engines, 820 silos, and 440 cream separators. Nearly every farm had a car, but only 1,430 had telephones and 1,150 had electricity.

Thanks to the hard work of Franklin County farmers as the Great Depression was beginning to take hold, Franklin

Secrets of Franklin County

County ranked first among Pennsylvania's sixty-seven counties for its peach and rye production, second for wheat and apple production, third for corn production and number of horses, fifth for its number of swine and wool production, seventh for barley production, eighth for its number of sheep, ninth for number of chickens and tenth for egg production.

That proud agricultural tradition continues today with Franklin County ranking in the top five in the state for products like milk, cattle, apples, hay and eggs. Also, the farms now have more bathrooms than radios in them.

Getting Paid What He Was Worth

When was the last time you heard of a public official not only volunteering, but insisting that his salary be more than cut in half? When have you ever heard of it?

It was as rare in the 1950s as it is now. That's why when Waynesboro's assistant manager and treasurer did it in 1958, it was reported in newspapers around the country. It probably also made a lot of public officials hope that the people they served didn't expect the same thing from them.

"I feel you're paying me too much, it's not fair to me nor to the public," A. Stover Fitz told the Waynesboro Council on Jan. 20, 1958, as reported in *The Public Opinion*.

It was a frank admission from a long-time borough employee. Fitz's salary at the time was $4,000 a year, which is roughly $31,200 in today's dollars. To further put it in context, the average income for a man in 1958 was $3,700 a year, according to the U.S. Census Bureau.

So Fitz's salary was only 8 percent above the national average, but to reach that amount, he was filling two roles for the borough and collecting both of the salaries for those positions. He collected the borough taxes in his role as borough treasurer and as the assistant borough manager. He provided assistance and advice to the borough manager.

"Make my salary $1,800 a year as treasurer and forget about the assistant borough manager title," Fitz told the council.

He was willing to take a fifty-five percent pay cut and still perform the same duties. It wasn't that he was being magnanimous; Fitz simply believed that public service should be more a service than a job. Fitz had worked for the borough in various capacities for forty-nine years. He had begun his career with Waynesboro as a part-time secretary in 1909. He rose through the ranks to eventually become borough manager before slowing down a bit to become the borough's assistant manager and treasurer.

At eighty-one years old, Fitz wanted to enjoy his remaining years without having to feel the need to work all hours of the day to justify receiving two salaries.

"I want to feel free to work a half day when I feel like it, take a half day off for illness and to come in late when it's snowing," Fitz said.

Council President Harold J. Rowe praised Fitz for his integrity and said that he believed that even when Fitz was working half a day, the work he did was still worth $4,000 a year. Fitz was insistent, though. He pushed his position and eventually convinced the borough council. The councilmen voted to cut Fitz's salary "with reluctance."

George Washington Masonic Lodge Celebrates Two Centuries and More

While the George Washington Masonic Lodge in Chambersburg, Pennsylvania, wasn't the first lodge of the Free and Accepted Masons in Franklin County, it is the oldest, and on April 23, 2016, it marked two centuries of service in the county.

Lodge No. 79

The first Masonic Lodge in the county formed in 1800. General James Chambers, son of Chambersburg's founder, Benjamin Chambers, served as the Warrant Master. Over the next five years, the lodge met fifty-four times and then closed its doors, not having gotten a strong membership base.

This didn't end Freemasonry in the county, though. Men continued to travel great distances to meet and fellowship at other lodges. However, the rigors of long travel for a relatively short meeting grows old quickly, and a group of men petitioned for a new lodge to be formed in Chambersburg.

George Washington Lodge No. 143

In 1815, the Grand Lodge of Pennsylvania acted favorably on the petition and issued a warrant on January 15, 1816, to George Washington Lodge No. 143. The lodge was constituted on April 23, 1816, and the Masons began meeting at various locations around the town.

"The meetings were first held in the Franklin County Courthouse, but that was considered an inconvenience," said Mike Marote, a member of the George Washington Lodge. Another location where the Masons met was Capt. George Coffey's Inn, but no one is sure where that inn was located in town.

The George Washington Masonic Lodge in Chambersburg, Pennsylvania. Courtesy of the George Washington Masonic Lodge.

The Masons purchased land for their temple in April 1823 and Silas Harry, a bridge builder, set the work to build the temple for $2,500. The final structure was a two-story brick building that was thirty-two-feet wide by sixty-seven-feet long. The foundation stone was laid on June 24, 1823, and the building was occupied on September 16 of the following year.

The 1830s saw a period where Masons were persecuted in the country, and the George Washington Lodge decided on December 3, 1830, "to go dark" as Lodge Worshipful Master Kevin Hicks said. The charter was returned to the Grand Lodge in 1831, essentially disbanding the lodge, but the Masons still met quietly and out of the public eye.

During this time, the Masons didn't own the temple, and it was used as a church printing office. The lodge reconstituted itself in 1845, but it wasn't until 1860 that the George Washington Lodge could repurchase the temple for $2,000.

The burning of Chambersburg

When Confederate General Jubal Early demanded a ransom from Chambersburg in 1864, the people weren't able to pay it. Early ordered the town burned, and $1.7 million in property was lost in the resulting flames.

One area of the town was left untouched, though. The Masonic temple, and the buildings in the half-block area surrounding it were unscathed.

"Confederate soldiers were posted out front preventing other Confederate soldiers from burning the lodge," Marote said.

The reason for this is that as the orders were being given to burn Chambersburg, an unnamed Confederate officer saw the lodge and took steps to save it. The surrounding buildings were also preserved because they were so close to the temple that if they had burned, they might have caught the temple on fire.

"Because the temple wasn't being burned, women and children were able to take shelter inside," Hicks added.

Since the officer was never identified, the story is considered a well-authenticated legend. Many of the other details have been verified and the half block around the temple was left untouched while the town burned around it.

Teachings

While there is much fellowshipping among the Masons, there is also instruction. Masons learn various speeches, passwords, and signs to move through 33 different degrees. Hicks noted that a man becomes a Master Mason at the third degree, though.

"We are learning what I call moral lessons with allegories," Hick said.

Though generally believed to be a Christian group, Masons include many faiths. The one requirement is that Masons must believe in a higher being. Each lodge has a book of faith on its central altar. The George Washington Lodge uses a Bible that is over 100 years old, but other lodges can include a book of faith for the predominant religion of the lodge.

"Freemasonry is not a church," Hicks said. "I look at it as a steady moral compass. You treat people like you want to be treated."

Masons are involved in many civic activities and participates in parades and building dedications. They can be identified in full regalia that includes tuxedos, top hats, and aprons.

"We have a belief in working for the greater good and for the good of the community," Hicks said.

Although the teachings are private matters for Masons,

the public has occasionally been invited in to witness these meetings.

Hicks would also like to open the temple up, on occasion, for artists to come in and use their time in the temple for inspiration for their art. He would then set up the social room as an art gallery where the artists could sell their works one evening.

A modern picture of the George Washington Masonic Lodge in Chambersburg, Pennsylvania. Courtesy of the George Washington Masonic Lodge.

Other lodges

Franklin County currently has three other Masonic Lodges: Acacia Lodge No. 586 in Waynesboro, Mount Pisgah Lodge No. 443 in Greencastle, and Orrstown Lodge No. 262 in Orrstown. A fourth lodge, Gen. James Chambers Lodge No. 801, merged with the George Washington Lodge to make both lodges stronger.

The George Washington Lodge boasts a membership of around 800 Masons.

200 years

To celebrate its bicentennial year, the George Washington Lodge hosted a luncheon and rededication of the cornerstone of the original lodge on August 23, 2016. Oddly enough, as of August 2015, the lodge was still unsure where the original cornerstone was located.

Chambersburg's Trolley Days

At the turn of the twentieth century, automobiles were a rarity that few people could afford. If someone needed to go to Chambersburg, Pennsylvania, from one of the nearby communities or get around town, he or she needed to ride a horse or walk.

That changed in 1902, as preliminary work began on planning a trolley route to service Chambersburg, but not one that was pulled by horses. The Chambersburg and Gettysburg Street Railway Company would be independently powered trolleys that would run from Chambersburg to Gettysburg.

The *Public Opinion* reported that, "Mr. Baumgardner declared it was so cold in December 1902 when surveying was done in the open country for the line that 'we had to cut the ground with an ax before we could drive an iron pin in.'"

The plan was eventually for the trolley line to run to Caledonia Park and then to push onto Gettysburg, Pennsylvania. The right of way for the trolley line was purchased, but no track was laid along it. Civil engineer Crosby Tappen would actually walk along the right of way from Caledonia to Gettysburg once a year to preserve the company's legal right for the path.

Workers began laying track in 1903. "The first section of trolley track in the borough ran onto the Wilson College campus but it never served any practical purpose, according to Joseph P. Turbridy, who supervised the laying of this initial track," according to the *Public Opinion*. The line ran north-south along Main Street through Chambersburg and formed a loop on the south end of town. The return line ran along Second Street. The line branched at Main Street at Queen Street and ran out to Caledonia Park.

Steve Emery of Bethlehem, Pennsylvania, built the trolley for a company of investors headed by J. M. Runk, a real estate dealer.

Trolley tracks being laid in Chambersburg, Pennsylvania. Courtesy of the Franklin County Historical Society – Kittochtinny

On August 14, 1903, the trolley was ready to run. "Chambersburg was alive with people last night. It seemed that the whole town had turned out to Main Street. There was something to bring them here, too..." the *Public Opinion* reported.

That grand opening caused more interest than a circus parade, according to the newspaper. An estimated 1,500 people took advantage of being able to ride the trolley for free that first day.

The trolley quickly became a popular form of transportation. Families would ride an open trolley car out to Caledonia in the summer for a picnic lunch while the children played on the playground. Also, every Saturday night, there was a dance at the park pavilion.

Two other trolley lines were soon built. The Chambersburg and Shippensburg Trolley and the Chambersburg, Greencastle and Waynesboro Company connected Chambersburg to its neighbors to the north and south.

Getting out to the park could be difficult at times, though. The Chambersburg and Gettysburg Trolley needed to cross the tracks of the Cumberland Valley Railroad at two points. However, the railroad company saw the trolley as competition and wouldn't allow the trolley a right of way across the tracks.

"One car ran to Third St., a second from Third to West Fayetteville and a third from there to Caledonia. Patrons had to walk across the railroad tracks at both transfer points," according to the *Public Opinion.*

Not only did this affect the passengers, but the calls themselves. If a trolley car further away from Chambersburg needed repairs, it had to be taken across the railroad line and set on the trolley tracks on the other side of the line.

The Cumberland Valley Railroad purchased the Chambersburg and Gettysburg Trolley in March 1905. Once this happened, the trolley could then cross the track and passengers could ride straight through to Caledonia. In later years, riders could get a transfer to a bus if they wanted to continue on to Gettysburg.

However, automobiles continued to grow in popularity, which reduced ridership on the trolley. At its peak, riders could catch a trolley in Chambersburg every fifteen minutes, but by the 1920s, the company began making cuts in service. The trolley company went from using double truck trolley cars to smaller single cars.

The last trolley left Caledonia Park on December 21, 1926. The Chambersburg, Greencastle and Waynesboro trolley and the Chambersburg in Shippensburg trolley both ended service at the end of July in 1928 and the service to Rouzerville, Pennsylvania, ended on January 16, 1932.

Hairy Memories

Charlie Chaplin wrote in his autobiography, "Hair is vitally personal to children. They weep vigorously when it is cut for the first time; no matter how it grows, bushy, straight or curly, they feel they are being shorn of a part of their personality."

It is a feeling that adults must never entirely get over, either. How many of us have scrapbooks that contain a lock of our hair from when we were a baby or when we got our first haircuts? When you look at it does it bring back memories of your childhood? Of a time of youthful energy and innocence?

Ann Hull, director of the Franklin County Historical Society - Kittochtinny, tells a story of how she was doing genealogy research one time and among some family items, she found an envelope with a lock of hair in it. "It wasn't labeled," says Hull. "I have no clue who it belonged to. It could have been from my great-grandmother. I could have been from my aunt. I don't know, but I wish I did to have that part of her."

"Hair, detached from its original owner, could nevertheless stand in for that individual. Emotional repercussions that would otherwise be the result of the interaction between individuals could be triggered by the hair itself," Helen Sheumaker wrote in *Love Entwined: The Curious History of Hairwork in America*.

Hairbooks

Before these scrapbooks with locks of hair, there were hair albums.

"They were before photography became common," says Hull. "This is how people remembered family and friends... with hair."

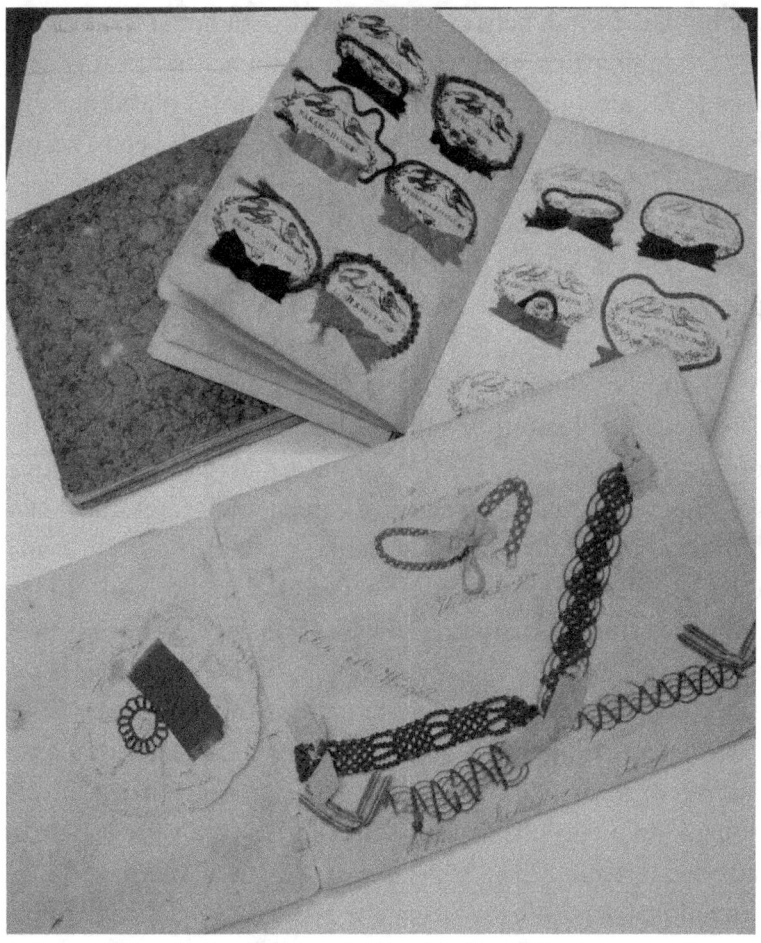

An example of the hairbooks at the Franklin County Historical Society – Kittochtinny. Author photo.

The Leila's Hair Museum in Independence, Mo., has six hair albums among its collection of hair art. Each has its own story that Museum Director Leila Cohoon researched. For instance, one book belonged to a woman in New York. Based on where the book is from and the morbid drawings throughout the book, Cohoon deduced the book was kept by an inmate at the women's prison in the town. Each lock of hair in the book is from a person who came to visit her at the prison.

One thing that characterizes hair albums is the way that hair locks are presented. They don't simply contain locks of hair taped into a scrapbook. These locks have been twisted into small braids and patterns.

"They're not braided in ways that we know braiding today," Cohoon said. The braids and weaving are more complex than the braids used nowadays.

Each lock is also identified with the name of the person to whom it belonged and sometimes a date or memory.

"It is a collection of intricate hair that was braided, embroidered, or woven and stitched into an album. Each sample has a tribute, usually a poem, done in beautiful, but faded calligraphy. It is dated 1865. It has two samples per page and there are over 80 individuals represented in the book. Many have the same last names. The hair of married couples is usually woven together," wrote a woman on the Victorian Hairwork Society about a hair album that she inherited.

The crafted hair lock might also be identified with a mini portrait or a verse of poetry. However it was identified, it was done so in a way that meant something to the young woman who was creating the hair album. A woman wrote in 1834, as quoted in *Love Entwined*, that she had "always loved albums, much as they have been ridiculed... and it interests me to see the ardour of a young lady, when opening the gilt leaves, she finds there sentiments dedicated to her alone."

Family Bibles have also been used as hair albums with locks of hair for each member of the family.

Most hair albums come from the nineteenth century, though other hairwork dates back much further. Cohoon says that young women making hair albums had pretty much ended by the beginning of the twentieth century.

Samples from the hairbooks and the names of the people from whom the hair came. Author photo.

"It's genealogy done with hair," Cohoon said.

In their book *Forgotten Tales of North Carolina*, Tom Painter and Roger Kammerer note that hair albums were quite popular in the state in the late 1880s, though even by then, it had begun to shift away from the more-labor intensive braiding. "The lock of hair would be tied with a blue ribbon and attached in an album. Over it would be written the name, age, eye color, date of receiving the memento and other personal remarks, which might or might not be complimentary, as the album was never to be seen by any other than feminine eyes," Painter and Kammerer wrote.

As photography became more commonplace, the tradition of keeping hair albums all but died out. It eventually morphed into the keeping of locks of hair and maintaining of hair work or the crafting of jewelry from locks of hair.

Hairwork

Hair albums are part of a larger art form known as hairwork. Hairwork involves using hair to create wreaths, rings, brooches, and other items. Learning hairwork involves skill that is learned.

Cohoon teaches classes in making hair wreaths. She has identified thirty techniques used in creating these wreaths. Cohoon knows twenty-five of them and is working to learn a twenty-sixth technique.

She has to figure them out herself because no directions on these skills exists. This has led her to write a book that provides instruction for how to do the various hair braids and weaves.

The benefit of using hair as a craft medium is not only that it provides a personal connection to the piece, but it does not decay.

"Everybody has hair," Cohoon said. "It's individual. It's the one part of the body that does not go back to 'dust to dust.'"

Beginnings

An article in *AntiqueWeek* by Susan and Jim Harran noted that hair has been seen as a symbol of life by many cultures over thousands of years. "Egyptian tomb paintings portray scenes showing pharaohs and queens exchanging hair balls as tokens of enduring love. In Mexico, Indian women kept hair combings in a special jar which was buried with their bodies so that the soul would not become tired looking for missing parts, and delay its passage to the other world," the Harrans wrote.

Cohoon said that she has seen hairwork traced back to the twelfth century. "Some people think of hairwork as something that was done during the Victorian era, but actually it was finishing up by then," Cohoon said.

As a commercial enterprise, hairwork is said to have begun in Sweden in the early 1800s. Young girls in Vamhus, Dalarna, Sweden learned creative hair braiding and then traveled far and wide earning money that helped support their village during the winter months.

"Young girls would divide up into teams of three or four and travel to a country in Europe, learn the language and take their art with them," the Harrans wrote. "The craft of hairwork spread throughout Europe. Beautifully detailed landscapes and floral designs were made by jewelers using human hair."

Acknowledgements

I wanted to thank all of those people who helped me put the *Secrets of Franklin County* together. The longer I work as a writer, the more I realize that while one person may publish a book, the effort is much richer when others assist.

I've been writing articles about the history of this region for nearly two decades. I've been doing the Secrets books for six years. I'm surprised it took me so long to get around to doing *Secrets of Franklin County*. Just goes to show you how many projects I have going.

One great local resource for finding the stories in this book was the microfilm files at the Coyle Library in Chambersburg, Pennsylvania, and the Alexander Hamilton Library in Waynesboro, Pennsylvania. I also found the local history room at the Hamilton Library the source of a few ideas that I pursued. The Franklin County Historical Society – Kittochtinny in Chambersburg was also a wonderful resource when I was originally writing the articles that make up the chapters in this book. For more information about Franklin County, pay them a visit or check out their website at www.franklinhistorical.org.

Finally, I'd like to thank Grace Eyler with E Plus in Emmitsburg, Maryland, for not only another great-looking cover but also being able to create the template for the Secrets series.

I have probably missed someone who I'll remember after this book goes to print. If so, it's not because I didn't appreciate your input. I sometimes get confused juggling all of the projects that I do. If I did leave you out, mention it to me. Meanwhile, I'm off to work on my next project.

James Rada, Jr.
March 1, 2023

About the Author

James Rada, Jr. is an Amazon.com bestselling author of historical fiction and non-fiction history. They include the popular books *Strike the Fuse, Canawlers,* and *Battlefield Angels: The Daughters of Charity Work as Civil War Nurses.*

He lives in Gettysburg, Pa., where he works as a freelance writer. James has received numerous awards from the Maryland-Delaware-DC Press Association, Associated Press, Maryland State Teachers Association, Society of Professional Journalists, and Community Newspapers Holdings, Inc. for his newspaper writing.

If you would like to be kept up to date on new books being published by James or ask him questions, he can be reached by e-mail at *jimrada@yahoo.com.*

To see James' other books or to order copies on-line, go to *www.jamesrada.com.*

PLEASE LEAVE A REVIEW

If you enjoyed this book, please help other readers find it. Reviews help the author get more exposure for his books. Please take a few minutes to review this book at *Amazon.com* or *Goodreads.com.* Thank you, and if you sign up for my mailing list at *jamesrada.com*, you can get FREE ebooks.

WANT TO KNOW MORE SECRETS?

Find out the little-known stories and hidden history of Maryland and Pennsylvania with the Secrets series from James Rada, Jr.

Available wherever books are sold.

www.ingramcontent.com/pod-product-compliance
Lightning Source LLC
Chambersburg PA
CBHW072005070526
44583CB00015B/1347